'Frank Furness has worked with some of the top performers in the business world and his experiences have made for a fascinating book. *Walking with Tigers* is filled with insights and no-nonsense charm – a must-read for anyone who wants to find their own path to success.'
Mike Southon, co-author of *The Beermat Entrepreneur*

'I really enjoyed reading this book, as it reminded me so much of things that I have tried to do in my life and the way I live. Frank's story is put in such an excellent way, with huge empathy and enthusiasm . . . I think all people who want to become 'tigers' could learn so much from Frank, and the lighthearted yet in-depth thinking he has put in this book.'
Raymond Ackerman, founder of Pick 'n Pay Stores

'*Walking with Tigers* is a great guide, helping you to be clear about what you want, take what you have in life, and move you to where you want to be!'
Amanda Gore, international speaker and author of *You Can Be Happy*

'Every time I sit in Frank's audience it's like going to the bank – and making a big deposit. What do you need to learn to fatten your bank account?'
W. Mitchell CSP, author of *It's Not What Happens to You, It's What You Do About It*

'Frank is one of the top sales presenters in the world and he delivered his high-content, high-impact, high-value presentation with his usual eloquence, expertise and enterprising nature.'
Dave Rogers, President, Asia Professional Speakers Association, Singapore

'Don't listen to Frank unless you plan on using at least some of his many incredible moneymaking ideas. If you listen and you don't act, it will lead to pure frustration.'
Scott Friedman CSP, President of the National Speakers Association USA, 2004–2005

'Frank brings tips and tools that can be applied no matter where one is on the rung of experience.'
Shelley Sykes B.Sc.(IT); MBA; Dip. Psych; Dip. Journ; CSP Australia

Frank Furness CSP hails from South Africa and is now a motivator, trainer and professional speaker based in London. He has 21 years' experience as a sales consultant, trainer and senior manager and has twice qualified for 'MDRT Top of the Table' (the top 0.5 per cent of salespeople in the world).

Frank is one of 500 speakers worldwide who has qualified as a Certified Professional Speaker. In November 1997 in Ireland, Toastmasters International recognised him as one of the top five humorous speakers in the UK. In August 2001 he was the only non-American listed in the USA *Meetings & Conventions* magazine as being one of the 10 most sought-after speakers on the professional speaking circuit. He is in great demand as a motivational and high-content speaker and is the past president of the Professional Speakers' Association of Europe.

He has been a guest on many radio talkback shows in the UK, speaking on goal setting, motivation and positive mental attitude. In 2002 his interview on Bloomberg TV about motivation for footballers in the World Cup was shown five times in 86 countries.

Frank started his motivational speaking, training and development company in 1997 and is currently working with many blue-chip companies. He brings a combination of high content and motivation to his talks, which he customises for each client. He has spoken in 48 countries and currently spends 70 per cent of his time abroad. He has clients from Russia to Hong Kong, Dubai to Malaysia, including the British Olympic team.

Walking
with
Tigers

Success Secrets from the
World's Top Business Leaders

FRANK FURNESS

PIATKUS

PIATKUS

First published in Great Britain in 2007 by Piatkus
This paperback edition published in 2009 by Piatkus

A CIP catalogue record for this book
is available from the British Library

ISBN 978-0-7499-4117-8

Edited by Andrew John
Text design by Goldust Design

Printed in the UK by CPI Mackays, Chatham, ME5 8TD

Papers used by Piatkus are natural, renewable and recyclable
products sourced from well-managed forests and certified
in accordance with the rules of the Forest Stewardship Council.

FSC

Mixed Sources
Product group from well-managed
forests and other controlled sources
www.fsc.org Cert no. SGS-COC-004081
© 1996 Forest Stewardship Council

Piatkus
An imprint of
Little, Brown Book Group
100 Victoria Embankment
London EC4Y 0DY

An Hachette UK Company
www.hachette.co.uk

www.piatkus.co.uk

Contents

Dedication

This book is dedicated to my mother and father, Susan and Malcolm, who encouraged me in everything I endeavoured (especially my mom who has been pushing me for years to write a book), my wife Candice for putting up with my travels and making me feel like the most special person on earth, and my son Jared who always encourages, challenges, teases and has fun with me. He also keeps me in some form of shape by taking me to the gym and pushing me to my limits.

Acknowledgements

Thank you to all the tigers who have contributed to make this book possible, people from all over the world, from as far as Australia, South Africa, Hong Kong, Japan, Canada, America, the United Kingdom, Thailand, Dubai, the Philippines, Malta and many other countries.

Thanks to Karen Farrington for the endless hours of help in the editing of this book.

Introduction

When it comes to business some people have a Midas touch. It's not just that they are wealth creators – although that's laudable enough – but they leave the golden glow of outstanding all-round achievement on everything they handle. For them business is pleasure and they generously spread their own feel-good factor among the rest of us. These people are tigers, named after the sleek, efficient and awesome operators of the jungle. They aren't plentiful in number, but they stand out from the crowd.

Not everyone in the hard-edged world of business is the same, however. The commercial landscape is littered with the wreckage of failed companies, their directors left scratching heads, wondering what went wrong. In addition, there are wannabes who aspire to the big time but flounder in a rut.

Like them, I've been intrigued by how and why events have unfolded so that some people are exalted while others are merely mundane. More specifically, I wanted to know about the qualities that tigers possess that are missing in the rest of the population.

After years of observing tigers at work I decided to carry out research to help define just what it takes to be a business tiger. During a speaking tour of ten countries around the world, I asked sales consultants to write down ten points that underpinned their success. I used my ever-expanding international database to field the same query to hundreds of other top-flight performers. Then I separated the responses into two piles, those from 'average Joes' and those from tigers.

From my findings I compiled this book, which encapsulates everything I've learned about tigers, flagging up just what elevates them above the norm. It's not just about business acumen – although that can be essential. The league table of necessary qualities thrown up by my research was topped by persistence, an attribute that can be honed in anyone. Persistence tended to go hand in hand with the desire to succeed, and it's hotly followed by the redoubtable duo of honesty and integrity. *Belief* and *focus* were two words that cropped up on numerous occasions, as did *attitude* and *confidence*. Perhaps knowledge and sales technique are obvious pointers to success, but personal discipline and organisation are less so. Other qualities that tigers exhibit in abundance are enthusiasm, listening skills, hard work and friendliness.

The result isn't rocket science, but it may be the formula that will help you mimic vital characteristics that will kick-start your career. It is designed to help you switch into a higher gear so you can quickly reach an enviable cruising speed. You get out of life only what you put in and no office behaviour bible is going to change that. But this will help you target your efforts to achieve the best results. See the graph opposite with the results of the research.

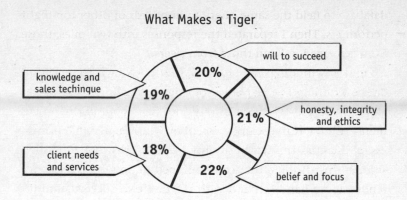

What Makes a Tiger

- will to succeed — 20%
- honesty, integrity and ethics — 21%
- belief and focus — 22%
- client needs and services — 18%
- knowledge and sales techinque — 19%

Chapter 1

My Story

Loud and frantic hammering on the front door woke me from a peaceful, dreamless sleep. It was 4 a.m. but instantly I could tell there was mayhem outside with sirens wailing and dogs howling. I peeped around the bedroom door to see a neighbour talking urgently with my father.

The ground had opened up and swallowed a neighbouring property, he said. Our family home was now teetering on the edge of a giant crater. 'Quick, you've got to get out!' he cried.

The groaning and shrieking from the structure of our home rang in our ears. The sight of wall cracks spreading like blackened lightning bolts in response to ominous earth tremors made us move fast. I grabbed my most treasured possession, a comic collection, and, dressed only in pyjamas, I headed for the car. Even as we drove away it seemed the fractured road might collapse beneath the car wheels. It was a few days after my ninth birthday – and my life had changed for ever.

My father had been an electrician in the gold mine at Blyvooruitzicht, a small gold-mining village two hours away from Johannesburg in South Africa. Every day he entered a wire cage and descended several miles through the Earth's crust to work in hot, cramped shafts. He laboured alongside men from all over Africa and spoke Fanigalo, the common language miners learn, whatever their background, to ensure safety and communication underground. Meanwhile, my mother stayed at home, taught piano and stitched clothes for my three sisters and I.

On Saturdays everyone in the village went down to the club to watch the local soccer and rugby teams in action and afterwards the men got involved in some serious drinking while the rest of the family watched a movie in the clubhouse. It was a remarkably close-knit community where there was little or no concern for the future. With housing provided by the company, miners tended to splash their cash on entertainment, furniture and holidays. Each week they saved some money towards the big Christmas celebration, which included a show, food, games and presents. Every year, as we stood in awe around the giant decorated Christmas tree, I remember people commenting on how beautifully my sisters were dressed.

For a young boy like me village life was a joy. I had freedom to roam and friends aplenty. We lived a contented but simple life.

But the village was built on dolomite, which soaked up rainwater like a sponge. We grew used to the idea of houses dropping a few inches into the ground after some low-grade subsidence. Sink holes were something else, though.

The home that had plunged some 50 metres (160 feet) into the ground belonged to Johannes and Hester Oosthuizen and their three children. Rescuers thought they could still see the roof of the house in the crater. In fact, that belonged to another building that tumbled in after it. The Oosthuizens would have died immediately, we were told later. Attempts to retrieve the bodies were abandoned because the area was unsafe.

That chaotic and highly charged night was the last we ever saw of our house, our possessions and our friends, as the village was quickly cordoned off and remained that way, so it became like a ghost town. Miners were used to danger on a daily basis, but, with their families now at risk, plenty like my father decided to leave the area for good. The garage belonging to my best friend's family disappeared into the earth. Although my best friend was safe, I never saw him again after that night.

We drove for two hours to my grandparents' place. Of course, my parents were now penniless with no possessions. We lived there for some time until my parents could afford a small deposit on a house. It proved a challenging task. My father tried to get work at the local mines, where my grandfather was a cage operator, but there were no vacancies. Hard-pressed for money, he took a job working as a sales representative for an electrical-goods company. Although he had never sold anything before and had a lot to learn, he persevered. My mother continued to teach children the piano and at the same time worked as a book-keeper.

If our family were poor either before or after the sinkhole disaster, I certainly didn't feel I missed out. I have great memories of my childhood, especially our family holidays. We packed up and headed for Margate, named from the resort in Kent, England, but our destination had acres of sand and an azure sea, and was drenched in hours of sunshine. Every morning fishermen used to gather up the sharks that had become caught up in the nets that protected the beaches. Occasionally you did hear about a shark attack, but I never gave a thought to the risks and plunged into the rolling waves at every opportunity.

One year that I remember vividly was when we were so hard up we slept in our car. In the mornings we would go to the public bathrooms, brush our teeth and shower and then spend the day on the beach and sleep in the car again that night until my folks found a couple of rooms for the rest of the holiday. It was really exciting to live like this for us as children. Another holiday at the seaside that sticks in my mind was when we slept in the back of a furniture shop owned by my dad's friend, who allowed us to stay there for nothing. So, even when times were tough, we never missed our annual holiday.

And I always had a school uniform, even though it was bought at the second-hand school shop and the sleeves were sometimes a bit short.

My mom – always bright and creative – went on to become an accountant for a number of companies while at the same time bringing in extra income by making soaps, candles and porcelain dolls. Meanwhile, my dad had gone on to become a top sales representative. Still they were casting around for a better way of life.

When they were both 48, my parents decided to launch their own business from home, operating as electrical wholesalers. They borrowed R2,000 (about £500 at the time) from the bank and my uncle lent them an old truck to get started.

On the first morning in business my father drove to the local gold mine to meet with the buyers and engineers. But, when he arrived, there was panic and chaos, because a vital part in the machinery had broken down. It brought production to a standstill and was costing the mine millions.

Everyone was too busy to speak to my father, but he gathered what the problem was, and that it would take several days for the new part to arrive. My dad's experience back in Blyvooruitzicht enabled him to summon up an alternative supplier. Quickly, he jumped in the truck and headed there. He was in luck. The supplier had the part that was needed. The only problem was, my dad had no cash. Thinking on his feet, he asked if he could have credit and fortunately the supplier took pity on him and agreed.

Back he dashed to the mine and saved the day. My dad became a hero and the future of his business was assured. His experience in mines allowed him to speak to almost anyone within the industry, helping them to solve problems and, at the same time, supplying electrical goods. This, combined with my mum's business brain and accounting skills, allowed their business to flourish and eventually move to large premises with staff. It became a well-established and highly respected enterprise. We finally had to force my father to sell the business when he was 73 years old, due to his health problems. My parents loved that business and ran it with passion and enthusiasm, treating their clients like gold. To me they are, and will always be, my most admired example of 'tigers'.

* * *

If the sinkhole at Blyvooruitzicht did one thing for me, it ensured I would not spend years in the mines as my father had done. Let me tell you a little bit about my background and how I became involved with some of the tigers in our industry.

When I was at school, I was average at academic work and sport and I was very much below average when it came to girls. No matter how hard I studied or how much work or effort I put in, I found that I only achieved standard marks. When it came to sport, I was the first one at every practice, grafted more than every other player on the pitch but always found myself picked to play in the second team. I wanted to hang around with the guys playing in the first team because they always seemed to attract the girls, but they didn't want to know me. I was too average to be part of their circle (I looked like a nerd, but without the brains).

After I left school I studied accountancy in the evenings and at weekends while working for an accounting firm by day, but once again found that I was just a mediocre student and I was constantly looking for something more. Soon I resigned and turned a hobby into a job by becoming a professional drummer. For the next six years I had the most wonderful time, travelling all over South Africa, Botswana, Gaberone, Maseru and Swaziland, and working alongside some of the top musicians and entertainers in that part of the world. I put in the practice and effort that was needed, drumming for two hours by myself every day, and soon became one of the most sought-after drummers in South Africa.

At the age of 26, I met Candice, who is now my wife, and decided that I needed a real job, but didn't know where to start. I had the germ of an idea in mind, because one of the most successful people I'd ever met was the man who had sold me two endowment policies and a retirement plan. He was Lincoln Myburgh, who was about 35 years old and drove a convertible Mercedes. Once, he invited me to his house to deliver some documents and when I got there I was amazed. Sited in about two acres of ground by a lake, the place seemed fit for a prince. Inside, he had a huge bar with a full-size snooker table, a swimming pool and, to my joy, a full-size squash court. Outside, he had his own yacht, catamaran and windsurfer. To me, he was truly an achiever. He was one of the first tigers I had encountered and I wanted to be just like him.

Back then he was manager of the local insurance agency and I asked if I could try out for the job of sales consultant. I had a haircut to get rid of the long locks I had grown as a musician, bought a suit and went for the interview. I was impressed with the branch. When I walked down the corridors, people were speaking about getting their Porsche serviced or going on holiday to Hawaii, and I knew that this was what I wanted to do. I wanted to be among the executives; I no longer wanted to be average.

As part of the interview I was given an aptitude test. The next day I received a phone call that shattered my dreams, I was told that the aptitude test showed that I would be no good for the life-insurance industry and that I should try another profession.

Well, I didn't want to go back to accountancy, so I begged the manager for a second chance. This time his boss, the regional manager, was there and for three and a half hours they grilled me. They phoned me a couple of days later and told me that the company employed only people with a proven success pattern. I had no past success pattern, as at the age of 26 my only possessions were a set of drums and an old van. In their eyes, I was below average and did not fit the mould of successful go-getter. Despite the rejection, I felt I could detect a chink of opportunity, so I didn't give up. I pestered senior staff and eventually, more out of desperation than anything else, they hired me.

I realised that, if I wanted to be a tiger, I had to mimic the style of the top salespeople. So I picked the elite producers in the branch, accompanied them on appointments, observed how they worked and how they lived and then tried to copy them, modelling my behaviour on theirs. To me it seemed an obvious course of action and I quickly achieved the desired results. In my first full year of selling I joined the top achievers at the branch.

Over the next thirteen years, I chiselled out a successful career in sales. Still, my ambitions had not been fulfilled and the desire to travel overseas loomed large.

In 1993, my family and I decided to move to London. I had three interviews lined up, the first of which was with a large, well-known organisation. When I met the chief executive he was puffing away on his cigar. I don't know whether that was supposed to impress me, but I have asthma and after a while my chest began to complain. Never once did he ask me if I minded the smoke. At the end of the interview I thought, well, I don't want to work for *this* man.

At the second interview the manager kept me waiting 20 minutes, although he knew I had just flown in from South Africa. He had his jacket off, his shirtsleeves rolled up, his tie loose, and I wondered whether this was the level of respect that he usually showed to staff and customers. After about five minutes he took a personal phone call and spoke for 15 minutes. Needless to say, I decided against working with *that* outfit.

The third company asked if I would work with existing staff members for a week, during which time I would be assessed. It would give me the chance to view the company from the inside as well as enabling the bosses to see what I could do, so I readily agreed to this commonsense option.

It was this company that I joined. It was a small practice with only two other advisers – I would become the third. This is one of the best decisions I have ever made, since these were two of the biggest producers in the insurance industry. They were truly tigers. Once again, I watched, learned from them and emulated what they were doing. This resulted in my qualifying twice for Million Dollar Round Table 'Court of the Table' and twice for Million Dollar Round Table 'Top of the Table' in my first four years in the UK. These are the highest accolades in the insurance industry and achieved only by the top 0.5 per cent of salespeople worldwide.

Although extremely successful in sales and sales management, I had long dreamed of starting up my own motivational speaking and sales training business. This way I could be working in collaboration with the greats, the true tigers of our industry, every day of my life. In 1997 I took that giant leap, moved away from my comfort zone and started the company. Through hard work, perseverance and some luck, everything went extremely well and I now work and speak in 48 countries around the world.

Looking back, I now realise how fortunate I have been to be surrounded by tigers. On my father's side:

- my grandfather, Frank Harold Furness, was an Olympic cyclist;

- my dad, Malcolm, played soccer for his state/county;

- my Uncle Trevor played soccer for South Africa;

- my Aunt Ruth started a business with her husband in a small flat, which grew into a multimillion-dollar international business.

On my mother's side:

- my grandfather was an amateur drummer who bought me my first set of drums and taught me to play;

- my mum, Susan, has the highest musical qualifications in piano and the very first band I played in was her dance band; she was also a finalist in the South African ballroom dancing finals;

- my sister, Susan, and her husband, Sava, started a bathroom accessory-importing business, which is now a multimillion-pound organisation;

- my sister, Daphne, and her husband, Peter, have a successful construction business;

- my sister, Cheryl, and her husband, Deon, have always encouraged their son, Brandon, at sport; now, at the tender age of 16, he plays major-league baseball, has been selected to play for South Africa and has been selected to play for his county/state at many other sports.

Of my family:

- my wife, Candice, is a successful entrepreneur: during our marriage she has had video, restaurant, catering and jewellery businesses and is now a partner in my business;

- my son, Jared, has a double honours degree in Portuguese and Spanish, also speaks French and Afrikaans and is now completing his law degree; he is also a qualified gym instructor.

If you are going to be thinking anyway, you may as well think big. Most people think small because they are afraid of success, afraid of making decisions, and afraid of winning. And that gives people like me a big advantage.

DONALD TRUMP

All our dreams can come true – if we have the courage to pursue them.

WALT DISNEY

When written in Chinese, the word 'crisis' is composed of two characters – one represents danger, and the other represents opportunity.

JOHN F. KENNEDY

Courage is being scared to death and saddling up anyway.

JOHN WAYNE

Attitude is a little thing that makes a big difference.

WINSTON CHURCHILL

Nothing in the world can take the place of persistence. Talent will not; nothing is more common than unsuccessful men with talent. Genius will not; unrewarded genius is almost a proverb. Education will not; the world is full of educated derelicts. Persistence and determination alone are omnipotent.

RAY KROC, MCDONALD'S PIONEER

Chapter 2

Dream Lovers

In dreams children can pursue their heart's desire. If they yearn to be a train driver or crane driver, pilot or pop star, well, it's no problem for them: they have the enviable ability to dream big. Only in adulthood do the boundaries descend like prison bars. These are the pernicious, self-imposed limits that can cage you in the dark recesses of an impenetrable box for the duration of your life. One of the keys to business success is retaining that childlike ability to have dreams with broad horizons.

One of the tigers I spoke to while I researched this book advised others to be audacious and 'believe that your dreams are possible'. It was vital, he said, to have sufficient imagination for dreams in the first place that will inspire you, those around you and eventually everyone around the world.

About seven years ago I started to work with a company called Meyado and its young, dynamic chief executive, Martin Young. Martin had a military background, having graduated at the prestigious Sandhurst Academy. His self-belief was matched only by his passion, set against the backdrop of a big dream. He had a small team of salespeople in the UK, four people in Germany and a similar number in Spain, but dreamed of offices worldwide and a reputation in financial services that was second to none.

Whenever I was with him his dreams and his enthusiasm were infectious. He believed that anything was possible and he had the discipline and perseverance to pursue his dreams. More than that, he managed to bring on board his employees, who began to share the vision. Seven years later, his sales force has increased tenfold and is spread among a network of offices across the globe. A multimillionaire, he has bought a steelworks in the US for $650 million and drives around in an Aston Martin. He spends the minimum time at work and makes the most of being at his farm with his family, playing with his children.

He sent me a paragraph of something he had written, and I often think about it.

> Have big dreams. Most people have a finite ability to work hard for so many hours each day and for so many years, with intense concentration. In my opinion, these people will fail to make an impact. Truly successful business people will live, breathe, sleep and dream about their business. These passions can't be manufactured. If you don't have the ability to be this passionate or are not fit enough to stand this pressure on your health or private life then change your industry or your goals. It will be cheaper for you in the long run.

No Limits

Having dreams and taking risks are two sides of the same coin. The greatest threat to modern society, in my view, is complacency and the dependence we tend to develop on security and comfort. The pioneers of yesteryear were not shackled in this way. They were willing to venture into the unknown and gamble their reputations in pursuit of a dream. They staked their health, wealth and even their safety on a seemingly insurmountable challenge. Not only were they willing to take risks, but they thrived on them. These were heroes who dared to break convention, defy common thought and possessed sufficient endeavour to shatter the paradigms to which their societies were rigidly attached.

Galileo flew in the face of an all-powerful papal authority when he insisted the earth travelled around the sun. Christopher Columbus discovered a new world for the Europeans when he embarked on a voyage into the unknown. Pioneering spirit is as valid and necessary today as it has always been.

I have contacted scores of tigers to discover just what motivates them. One of the first observations I made is that they are all visionaries. They have big dreams, are 'no-limit' people and are prepared to take risks that others wouldn't contemplate.

Tony's Story

New Zealander Tony Christiansen knows all about having big dreams. He has been a speedway driver, pilot, businessman, gold-medal-winning Paralympic athlete, an acclaimed surf lifesaver, martial-arts expert and mountaineer. All this when a railway accident at the age of nine left him without legs. He is also a father of three and grandfather of two.

Tony always had the vision to see beyond his missing limbs and expects others to do the same. He judges people by attitude rather than body shape. 'I had that no-fear attitude and the blind faith in myself that I could do anything. Ten foot tall and bulletproof,' he told me. 'I know many able-bodied people that are far more disabled than I will ever be.'

One of his first challenges after he lost his legs was learning to swim. Although he didn't previously much like water, two dedicated coaches taught him first to keep afloat, then to execute the strokes. 'I was the only kid at school who could swim a mile – and I had no legs.'

After realising the potency of goal setting at this early age, he went on to every new challenge undaunted. In short, he owned his own business by the age of 27, climbed Africa's highest peak, Mount Kilimanjaro, and represented New Zealand both in the Paralympic Games and in tae kwon do, in which he is a second-degree black belt. Add to that his love of go-karting – a sport in which he could compete on level terms as a youngster – and a pilot's licence and you get the picture of a remarkable man. But, he insists, it is his attitude rather than his disability that makes him different.

'We all have the capacity for greatness within us. We just have to take all the opportunities – and sometimes the risks – to reach the next step of the journey towards being the very best we can be.'

Rudy's Story

A few years ago in the USA, I met a man who became one of the nation's most unlikely heroes. His name is Daniel 'Rudy' Ruettiger and he is marked out among men by achieving what seemed to be an impossible dream.

The third of 14 children, Rudy was the son of an oil refinery worker, yet he always had the unlikely ambition of attending the prestigious Notre Dame University in Michigan. His family, friends and everyone he knew told him that he wasn't clever enough to attend university and that he should settle for something less. Mediocre grades in school seemed to back their case. So, instead of going to university, he joined the navy. However, away at sea he met a colleague who set him straight. 'If you want to go to university so badly, then go and do it.'

Inspired by those words, he went back to college to gain the necessary qualifications and was rejected from Notre Dame on numerous occasions before finally being accepted in 1974. At an age when most people had *completed* university, Rudy *began* his studies. He didn't care about the age gap that separated him and most other students, since this was the fulfilment of a dream he had always been told was impossible.

But his ambitions were not yet satisfied. His next target was to play football for Notre Dame, and this seemed beyond reach as Rudy stands only 1.7 metres (5 feet 7 inches) tall and weighs 75 kilos (165 pounds). Most of the others trying out for the team were around 2 metres (6 feet 5 inches) tall, with broad shoulders and barrel chests and numbered among the top college football players in America.

Yet this anomaly didn't stop Rudy from harbouring his dream. He was the first one at every practice and the last one to leave, giving 110 per cent on every occasion. If he got knocked down he would get up and go at it again. Derisory comments from other players came thick and fast but that didn't squash his enthusiasm. Although his ability was a little under par, Rudy's commitment was always beyond doubt.

In 1976 Rudy was about to qualify and Notre Dame were once again in the finals of a prestigious competition, playing Georgia Tech. Knowing the time and effort Rudy had given, the coach told him to kit up and stand on the sidelines. He wasn't good enough to play, but he had achieved the dearly held ambition of wearing the blue and gold of the 'Fighting Irish' and stand-ing among the elite. With two and a half minutes to go in the game, Notre Dame could not lose, so the coach sent Rudy onto the field. When Rudy tackled the quarterback from the opposing side the stadium erupted with chants of 'Rudy, Rudy, Rudy!', and he was carried off on the shoulders of his teammates, the only time such an event has ever happened. Never have the virtues of a number 45 been so extolled.

A problem with dreamers is that they never stop dreaming, and, as soon as Rudy had achieved this, he decided to make his story into a film. Once again, he was ridiculed, rejected and re-galed with reasons as to why no one would want to know about this two-minute window in American football history. Unde-terred, Rudy wrote the script and eventually, after astonishing perseverance, the film was made, starring Sean Astin and direct-ed by David Anspaugh.

Much later he was speaking publicly about his remarkable life when a boy from the audience asked, 'What was it like when you made that tackle?' The footballing action was merely a symptom of a far greater game plan, Rudy explained. 'It wasn't about that tackle: it was about what I accomplished.'

At the same event a woman asked why he didn't listen to people who told him his dreams were out of reach. With poign-ant honesty, he admitted that he had a lot of anger inside caused by people telling him what he could and couldn't accomplish in life. He used that anger in a positive way to prove the doubters wrong.

Rudy has become the inspiration for countless thousands, in-cluding the actor Chris Burke. Chris, who was born with Down's syndrome, was also told the dice were loaded against him, that he was destined to fail. Nonetheless, he became an actor, got his own show and was a Golden Globe nominee for his role in the nineties American TV series *Life Goes On.*

'Rudy's dream was to play football at Notre Dame and I felt the same way about acting – I wanted to do my own TV show. What he did was remarkable. He is my hero. He never gave up, and that's his message,' Burke said.

I have met Rudy and seen the film, and I would advise anyone in search of inspiration for themselves, their family or their children to see the movie *Rudy* (1993). His fundamental rule for life is that persistence pays dividends. Whether it was football, school or work, he would never give up and always achieved what he set out to do.

Rudy sums his ethos up in two simple but memorable phrases. 'Dreams are what make life tolerable,' he says. And to those who have identified where their dearest ambitions lie he instructs, 'Just go get it.'

So start dreaming; start becoming a no-limit person. Dreams are the creative vision of your life in the future and help you design the life you want. Why dream small?

Don't waste a minute. It's time to write out your master dream list so do it now. Include on it everything you've ever wanted to have or be. Don't commit the cardinal error of imposing limits. If you find some boundaries creeping in then ask yourself, what is stopping you from becoming a no-limit person?

The indispensable first step to getting the things you want out of life is this: decide what you want.
BEN STEIN

In the middle of difficulty lies opportunity.
ALBERT EINSTEIN

Until you commit your goals to paper your intentions are like seeds without soil.
WINSTON CHURCHILL

I do not try to dance better than anyone else. I only try to dance better than myself.
MIKHAIL BARYSHNIKOV

Success is the progressive realisation of predetermined worthwhile goals.
PAUL J. MEYER

When you set goals, something inside of you starts saying, 'Let's go, let's go,' and ceilings start to move up.
ZIG ZIGLAR

Chapter 3

Go-Getter, Goal Setter

True tigers are also dedicated goal setters and achievers. They define objectives in all areas of their lives and keep written goals for the short, medium and long term in both business and personal life.

Early in my career I undertook a course on goal setting and since then it has become a passion. My personal list of aims and ambitions has been like a magic wand because, inspired and guided by my chosen goals, I've achieved everything I've wanted in life.

One of the things I enjoy most about what I do is working with top sports people. They all have great stories to share, so I teach them speaking and presentation skills for a life outside sport. When I am with them the room fizzes with energy, whether they are runners, swimmers, football players or Paralympians. To me, a key trait they all have in common is that they set and monitor goals to help make their dreams come true. It's not just that which beckons them to success, of course: they are also willing to learn, keen to be coached, are self-motivated and love the feeling of winning. But their structured approach is pivotal.

For Olympic athletes their stage is set only once every four years for an appearance that can often be measured in seconds. To be the best, they work out what they must achieve annually, then monthly, weekly and daily to structure their training in order to reach that pinnacle.

Take the super-achiever Sarah Bailey, who is the winner of 16 Paralympic medals, five of them gold, and the holder of 14 world records. She captained the Great Britain Paralympic team when it took part in the athletics World Championships in New Zealand in 1998 and the European Championships in Germany in 1999. After retiring from a successful career in swimming, she decided to try cycling and went on to bag more medals. Her dreams were big but she also set herself targets to ascend to the apex of success.

I asked her what it was like to stand on the winners' podium and hear her country's national anthem being played before receiving a gold medal at the Olympics. She told me to imagine all the happiest moments of my life and multiply by a million. It is that feeling of achievement and self-fulfilment that comes from setting and achieving goals.

Sarah said, 'There is no such word as *can't*. If you want to do something badly enough you can just go out there and do it. Life is a journey, follow your dreams and be happy in all that you do.'

Here are some words of wisdom from sports people I've worked with:

No matter what negative things occur to you, always draw from them the positives, and you keep moving forward.
Leon Taylor, diver

Don't be afraid to embrace the bad days because then you will get to appreciate the good ones.
Mark Ecclestone, tennis player

Believe in yourself every single day.
James Hickman, swimmer

If you have the three ds of dedication, determination and discipline you can reach the top.
Sacha Kindred, swimmer

Never be afraid to follow your dreams.
Helen Clitheroe, 1,500-metre runner

Having goals helps us translate our dreams into reality. They give us the privilege to choose how to invest our time and energy and help us to plan and take action. I've often questioned why some people don't set goals and have heard all kinds of excuses, including fear of failure, fear of success (strange as it may seem), a lifestyle that has so far not included goal setting and an unwillingness to leave the comfort zone.

Can you imagine what the world would be like if sports people didn't set goals, if businesses had no goals, targets or plans and if nobody set any personal objectives for themselves? And remember: goal setting is a highly personal project.

Personal Best

What I love about goal setting is that you are not measuring yourself against anyone else. It's a case of being the best you can be. And success means different things to different people. To some, success equates with wealth and material possessions. To others, it is the attainment of good health, peace of mind or a happy family life. In general, success can be defined as the continuous process of attaining your desired goals.

When I was at school, my best friend was from a very conservative family with a narrow outlook. He was bright and received top grades at school and university, so his family were very proud of him. Then he decided to become a Buddhist and went to live in robes in the mountains of Tibet. His was a frugal existence. He wore second-hand clothing and was dependent on food donations. Now the rest of his family were horrified: this was not part of their life plan for him at all.

He lived in Tibet for some time, met a lovely woman and married her. He is now back in South Africa working as a scientist. Most scientists don't make a lot of money, but that doesn't concern him. His goals are not about money: they are about spiritual fulfilment, good health and happiness. He never wakes up at two o'clock in the morning worrying about the pressures of work because he is at peace with his life. So we all have different goals and aspirations. Find out what it is that motivates you and follow that passion.

My own experience is a good advertisement for the value of goal setting. Years ago I was somewhat reluctant to buy a course on the subject. At the time it cost two months' salary and I didn't even know what goal setting was. But the salesman assured me it was all I needed to accomplish my dreams. I was really excited when I got the books and the tapes and spent hours absorbing the information – and that's an important part of the process. Goal setting is all about repetitiveness until the message is ingrained. It has got to become a habit. Anyway, I did as I was asked and noted down everything I wanted out of life.

One of the first goals that I wrote down was that in six months I was going to get a new Mercedes. This was to replace a clapped-out motor that I drove, which had a nasty habit of failing to start in the mornings. I got all the car brochures and put them up on the wall. My friends mocked me and I was a bit despondent, but the goal-setting course warned about the jealousy and criticism that you encounter when you set new challenges.

I worked out what I needed to buy that car on a month-by-month, week-by-week and day-by-day basis. Six months later I drove out of the dealership in it and I can still recall the smell of the leather that flooded my nostrils. I sank into the seat, feeling prouder than I had ever felt. All those who had teased and taunted me kept pretty quiet.

I had never been overseas, so I wrote down 'travel'. Once again people laughed and said it wouldn't happen. Undeterred, I went to the travel agency to work out a three-month itinerary and its cost. After I had established weekly targets, it was down to me to earn sufficient money to finance the venture. I knew I could make the difference. Working on commission, I saw people at all hours, seven days a week, knowing all the while what figures I had to meet to make my dream come true. I was really focused on this goal of going overseas. It came as no surprise to me when my wife and I boarded the aircraft for our first long-haul holiday.

First, we flew to London, then travelled all over Europe – and we had more fun than we had ever had. Then we went to America, where we visited Disneyland, before spending eight weeks touring the continent. We ended the adventure in Brazil.

In short, it was the holiday of a lifetime, one we have never forgotten.

With pure delight I realised I had achieved everything I had set down as a goal. I then realised the awesome power and the utter joy of goal setting. All you have got to do is have a dream, write it down and draw up an action plan that will take you where you want to be. Be realistic. At no point should your action plan include winning the lottery. Ideally, goals should be out of reach, so you stretch yourself to get there, but not out of sight. Write down what you have to do each and every day to get there. Then all you need is commitment.

I wrote to 500 top salespeople around the world. One of my findings was that they had written down specific goals. Goal setting jigsaws neatly with the twin characteristics of belief and focus that all possessed in abundance. Do you have written goals?

I love my job, I get the opportunity to travel, meet new people, encounter different cultures and speak about my passions, sales, technology and achievement. I work from home with my wife Candice, so we can work our own hours, go shopping when we want and take holidays whenever suits us. After I identified what I wanted from life, goal setting helped me achieve it. You must discover what it is that you really want out of life and then make it happen.

Taking Action

If you haven't already done so it's time to start goal setting, and here are some ways of getting started.

SETTING YOUR GOALS

1. Identify your goals.

2. Identify the benefits of achieving your goals.

3. Identify any obstacles you may have to overcome.

4. Will you have to acquire any new skills or knowledge to achieve this goal?

5. Will you have to work with any individuals, groups or organisations? If so, who?

6. What is the first thing you need to do?

7. Set yourself a time limit to achieve this goal (for example, next week, next month, next year, within five years).

Look first at financial goals and ask yourself why you are working and what you want to achieve. Consider where you would like to be in five and ten years' time or what you hope for before retirement. Note down anything that involves a major financial outlay, including car, family weddings and children's education. You are living without limits, so don't, therefore, put any restrictions on your earning potential or what you want out of life.

Then it's time to set physical goals, as modest as walking the dog or as ambitious as running a marathon. Perhaps you want to trim a centimetre or so from your waistline. If you already exercise and watch your diet, then consider pushing the boundaries. If you don't, then you know that you should, and now is as good a time to start as any.

After that, investigate family goals. Let's face it, you can re-place money at any time but it's impossible to recreate your family. Give plenty of quality time to your children. Before you know it, they will be out of the house and gone from your every-day life. All that will be left will be regrets that you didn't spend more time with them.

Social goals are important, too, and I've discovered that most tigers give something back to society either by coaching chil-dren in sport or contributing to charity.

Don't disregard mental goals and the challenge of lifelong learning. Remember that the top achievers in business continue their education even when their careers no longer depend upon it. So think about your mental goals, write down what areas of your life you think you should improve, and then start getting the specifics into place.

The last area is spiritual goals. This could be linked to a church, synagogue, temple or mosque – or indeed any aspect of organ-ised religion. But it might also be a case of simply getting back to nature and smelling the roses.

Goal setting is a highly individual process and your shopping list of success will be unique. You are the only person who can work out what truly makes you happy.

Be prepared to exert the energy, summon the effort and find the time needed to reach those goals. Where are you going to focus your energy, effort and time? You have got to work that out. It's a good idea to involve your family in the process, so everybody is aware of the evolving blueprint. Keep monitoring your goals, since they may change over time. You might succeed in some sooner than planned. Others might become irrelevant over time. But potential change is no good reason to sidestep goal setting.

Write it Down

Of course, the biggest secret of successful goal setting is putting pen to paper and writing down your aims in each of the allotted areas. Then put a date on it and formulate a plan of action to achieve these aims. Don't forget: they might be weekly, monthly or yearly in timescale.

Goals that stay in your head will live on only as mist-shrouded, unachievable dreams. Keeping them trapped in the nether reaches of your brain is a barrier to success. Do that and you will live life in the doldrums repeating the mantra 'I would have, I should have, I could have.'

There is almost something magical about taking a pen and writing that goal. We have all got a subconscious mind, and while you are sleeping it is working on the written goals you have set. I still set goals all the time.

Before you nod off you are in what is known as the *alpha state*, the time you are most receptive to new notions. After you've gone to sleep your brain gets to work on these targets, making the ground fertile for these seeds to grow. It also helps you to prioritise. Recent research has proved that while we sleep the brain goes to work, filing information passed to it that day. According to Bob Stickgold, professor of psychiatry at Harvard Medical School, 'We're not just stabilising memories during sleep: we're extracting the meaning.' It all makes focusing during the following day a whole lot easier.

In February 2007, Robert Adler, a US inventor best known for the creation of that dream device, the TV remote control, died at the age of 93. This was not his only invention. Together with fellow engineer, Eugene Polley, he notched up more than 180 US patents in a 58-year career. And he was a man who knew the value of a good night's sleep, during which he would crack some scientific conundrum.

His widow, Ingrid, said the remote was not his favourite invention, that he rarely watched television and was 'more of a reader'.

'He was a man who would dream in the night and wake up and say, "I just solved a problem,"' she told the Associated Press news agency. 'He was always thinking science.'

He produced the first remote control device, attached to the TV by a cord, in 1950.

High Definition

You have to be specific about your goals. Don't be lured into the vague or ill defined. If I said I really wanted to lose some weight, well, it doesn't amount to much in isolation. If I said I wanted to lose 5 kilos (11 pounds) in three months, it's possible to quantify and measure my goal.

For dieters a further extension to goal setting is keeping a note of every morsel that passes their lips and when. Note takers will lose much more weight than the rest, because they have a ready-made reality check at hand. Others tend to foster a skewed outlook – and wonder why the pounds or kilos stay in place.

I meet so many people who refuse to come out of their comfort zone and set foot into the world of goal setting. They think like conformists or average Joes. The winners in life don't put any limitations on their commitment to succeed. You are never too old or too young. It's up to you to create the right circumstances.

Joseph Stalin is remembered as an advocate of five-year plans. Although I'm usually more fussy about the company I keep, I have to agree with him on this, since it's an ideal way to frame your ambitions. A five-year plan is a clear and concise goal-setting guide to ultimate success. A lot of people are daunted at the prospect of dealing with large chunks of time. Some of you might ask, 'How can I prepare a five-year business plan when I don't know where I'm going to be in the future?'

Well, business plans are not written in stone. They can change, just as goals and general circumstances do. But a five-year plan gives you something to work with in the foreseeable future and helps keep you on message, fending off the aimless drift that might otherwise envelop your life.

One major problem in the business world is that most people are so busy fighting fires that they never get around to the most vital few activities that will lead to the greatest results. A five-year plan is a great way to identify and tackle these activities, and it's a one-way route to success.

Don't measure yourself against anyone else. Be the best that you can be. Have the best business you can. That is all life asks of you.

I did a lot of work with Panasonic some time ago, involving a one-day orientation to understand better how to work with the Japanese. We were told that the holding company Meichi has a 250-year business plan broken down into 20-year segments. It's a technique that's certainly worked for this corporation!

Here are a few tips on formulating your personal go-ahead five-year diary.

1. **Break down five years into 12-month segments so it is instantly easier to digest.**

2. Identify when you are taking your holidays. Holidays are important to top business people, so don't miss out. Plot the dates of conventions and so forth and put a year planner on your wall to ensure that priority events are always in sight. Now it's easy to see how much time is left available for business.

3. Decide on a production goal for the year, and dividing that total by the number of weeks left blank on the wall planner, discover your weekly goal. From this you should be able to deduce the number of deals you need to be closing on a weekly or monthly basis. Every business is different, of course, but using this formula gives you a timescale with which to approach your workload. Review your achievements every quarter to see if you are in line with predictions. In doing so you can work out your personal costings, which can be mind-blowing.

If you expect to earn	Each hour is worth	Each minute is worth	Your cost for wasting 1 hour per day per year
£50,000	£25	£0.42	£6,250
£75,000	£37.50	£0.63	£9,375
£100,000	£50	£0.83	£12,500
£150,000	£75	£1.25	£18,750
£175,000	£87.50	£1.46	£21,875
£200,000	£100	£1.67	£25,000
£250,000	£125	£2.08	£31,250
£350,000	£175	£2.92	£43,750

4. At the other end of the timescale, don't forget a daily to-do list that will keep you focused on the essentials at hand. Every night before going to bed, write down the six most important things you want to achieve the next day.

Here lies a man who attracted better people into his service
than he was himself.
ANDREW CARNEGIE, EPITAPH

Statistics suggest that when customers complain, business
owners and managers ought to get excited about it. The
complaining customer represents a huge opportunity for more
business.
ZIG ZIGLAR

There is less to fear from outside competition than from inside
inefficiency, discourtesy and bad service
ANON

I am easily satisfied with the very best.
WINSTON CHURCHILL

Chapter 4

People Power

All the tigers I've ever met have surrounded themselves with a close-knit team, hand-picked for will more than skill. For, no matter how adept, a businessman is only as proficient as those around him.

I came over to London in 1993. I was fortunate enough to be working with two tigers. Although only three of us were out there producing business, we had nine administrative and back-up staff. We paid them extremely well and, because of this, they were dedicated and loyal, and we had almost no staff turnover. They participated in the profits and we were all part of a working team. Only together were we able to reach our potential.

The right people come in all shapes and sizes – and ages. They are not necessarily young, good-looking and university-educated. My dad was 18 years old when he started his business. Did you realise Mozart composed his first work at the age of seven? Bill Gates, the richest man on earth, was 20 when he started Microsoft. But Ray Kroc, the driver of the McDonald's empire, began the company we know today at the age of 52. Ronald Reagan was elected president when he was 70 years old. Michelangelo painted the Sistine Chapel at 71 years old.

I spent many years building up a sales force in South Africa and reaped rewards by attending to three key areas: recruiting the right staff, retaining them and attaining the sales targets by motivation, coaching and encouragement. I feel these factors are just as relevant today with any organisation.

A Potent Brew

If anyone knows about the importance of this type of people power in business it is entrepreneur Karan Bilimoria, the founder of Cobra Beer. A Cambridge law graduate and qualified chartered accountant, Karan went into the brewing business when he realised Britain needed a smoother, less gassy beer that appealed to ale drinkers and lager drinkers alike, and one that would also complement all types of cuisine.

With no prior knowledge of the marketplace, Karan entered the most competitive beer market in the world opposite long-established, giant brands and at a very difficult time – the first shipment of Cobra was imported into the UK in 1990, at the start of a recession.

These days Cobra Beer is stocked in more than 6,000 restaurants and in most major supermarkets and off-licence chains in the UK. Cobra is also available to nearly 6,000 pubs, bars and clubs. It is now one of the fastest-growing beer brands in the UK, having been exported to almost 50 countries worldwide, and with subsidiaries in India, South Africa and the USA. The company continues to go from strength to strength with a compound annual growth rate of more than 42 per cent in the last 10 years.

Karan believes staff members are at the very foundation of this success story. 'Once you get your product right, the most important thing is people,' he told me. 'That is what is going to give you the competitive edge. In terms of recruitment I believe you have to keep an open mind. People in our company have come from a variety of sources – recommendations, advertisements or recruitment agencies.

'But the most important thing in looking for people is that it is better to hire for will rather than skill. Ideally, you hire for both, but if it's a choice I would rather have somebody with the right attitude. It's always the attitude that counts.'

When he recruits staff he puts his theories into practice. 'In 1993 we were a very new beer brand. My partner and I decided to recruit two salespeople. We advertised in London and got over one hundred applicants. We hired the two we were looking for but the person who came third desperately wanted the job. We explained he had missed out.'

Although the unlucky candidate didn't seem to possess the right credentials – at the time he was an asylum seeker from Pakistan and his English wasn't very good – something about his ambition impressed. Karan agreed to give him a chance and was duly rewarded for his sound judgement.

'He said he would do the job on a commission-only basis. We told him we had asked the other two salespeople to sell one hundred cases per week each within the month. He set off and achieved the target within two weeks, so we made him permanent. Today, he is Cobra's sales director and doing phenomenally. He will be a millionaire one day through share options alone.'

And he's not the only member of staff to climb rungs in the company, as Karan explains. 'About four years ago we had a South African girl who came in on a bicycle to sell sandwiches every day. We liked her and asked her to do telesales during the evenings.

'She was so good at the telesales that we persuaded her to give up selling sandwiches and to join us full time. She was so excellent at the job that she became manager of the telesales department within a year. From there she stepped in to the role of my head PA, and now she has become Cobra's first ever HR [human resources] manager.'

Asked what he would take to a desert island, Karan pays perhaps the ultimate tribute to his team. 'I would take my management team with me because I trust them implicitly. We get on well and have complementary skills.'

For Karan the formula for generating people power is simple: 'You create this environment where anyone can get to anywhere in the organisation.'

When I walk into the offices at Cobra Beer I can feel the people-power vibe. Everybody knows me and it's like walking into a happy family occasion. The story of Cobra Beer remains inspirational and Karan Bilimoria is a natural tiger because he had the belief to carry it through.

'I came up with the idea for Cobra when I was a student in Cambridge and London. Like most business ideas, it stemmed from being dissatisfied with a product or a service and thinking I could do it differently and better. Ideally, you feel you can change the marketplace you are going into.

'In my case I had an intense dislike for lagers in Britain, which I found bland, fizzy and difficult to drink. The experience of drinking lager with Indian food was very unpleasant. A friend of mine introduced me to real ale, which I love to this day, but it didn't take me long to discover that real ale and Indian food do not go together either.'

Karan's aim was to create a beer that was as refreshing as a lager but would also appeal to ale drinkers, one that was less gassy and a good accompaniment to Indian food. He started from scratch, creating a recipe and a brand.

'In 1990 we shipped out one container of beer from Bangalore [now Bengaluru] in India to the UK. It reached hundreds of containers a year by 1996, and the following year we moved brewing to Britain. Now we are brewing Cobra in Britain, Poland, Holland, Belgium and once again in India.'

His business principles from the outset have been and remain very straightforward:

- the product comes first;

- always strive to be different and better;

- never ask for exclusivity;

- treat suppliers and customers alike;

- maintain an informal yet professional office atmosphere.

He has learned some important lessons about business. 'When you are starting a business it is very tough. The first few years are incredibly difficult. Usually you are starting with limited resources. In fact, one of the definitions of entrepreneurship is coming up with an idea, having limited resources, having all odds stacked against you and going out there and making it happen.

'In those early years you have to cross what I call the credibility gap, where nobody knows you, your product or your service. You have got to persuade them to buy from you. And what is it that is going the make them do that? I believe if you have the absolute passion, faith and confidence in yourself and in your idea, then they will give you a chance.'

He underscores the importance of leading by example, being a doer and not just a thinker. 'Management is very much about execution. Leadership is about strategy, taking people with you and making them believe. It is the same as the difference between a mission and a vision.

'In the case of Cobra our mission is to brew the finest Indian beer and to make it a global beer brand. Its success is very measurable and you can check its progress. The vision is what underlies everything you do. In our case it is to aspire and achieve against all odds, with integrity. It is not just *what* you do: it's how you do it.'

So when you are recruiting staff you are well advised to look for individuality as much as hard work and for common sense alongside qualifications. Having the best team around you is worth a lot of money.

A Higher Plane

I read a great hint in the book *Nuts* by Kevin and Jackie Freiberg about Herb Kelleher and the successful American airline Southwest Airways. Kelleher said, 'Get the right people on the bus, the wrong people off, and only then can you start moving forward.'

He was one of the founders of the airline, which began with four planes and fewer than 70 employees in 1971 after a protracted legal battle with existing carriers. When it hit cash-flow problems early on, Southwest had the choice of either selling a plane or laying off employees. Unusually, the airline managers sold the plane. In return, the airline requested their employees cut gate turnarounds down to 15 minutes. The employees obliged, helping establish one of the friendliest management–labour relationships in the airline industry.

Staff members have been as big a priority as customers. Indeed, Kelleher credits Southwest's employees for the company's success. He says he simply hires the best people, treats them with respect and gives them the freedom to make decisions and to have fun just being themselves.

Everyone gets involved in the company profit-sharing scheme, which gives them added inspiration when it comes to customers. The airline insists, 'We are a great customer service organisation that just happens to be an airline.' Only the expertise of frontline staff can make this boast come true.

Kelleher has become famous for his offbeat corporate culture. In one outrageous incident in 1992, he staged an arm-wrestling showdown with the CEO of Stevens Aviation. Both Stevens and Southwest were using the advertising tagline 'Plane Smart'. To settle the matter, Kelleher suggested the competition, with the winner keeping the rights to the slogan. Kelleher lost, but the event generated so much goodwill and publicity that Stevens let Southwest continue using the tagline.

In 1997 he wrote an article in *Leader to Leader* magazine called 'A Culture of Commitment', which outlined his special approach to staff.

Our most important tools for building employee partnership are job security and a stimulating work environment. Our union leadership has recognized that we provide job security, and there hasn't been a lot of that in the airline industry. Certainly there were times when we could have made substantially more profits in the short term if we had furloughed people, but we didn't. We were looking at our employees' and our company's longer-term interests. And, as it turns out, providing job security imposes additional discipline, because if your goal is to avoid layoffs, then you hire very sparingly. So our commitment to job security has actually helped us keep our labor force smaller and more productive than our competitors'.

But it's not enough to try to assure people a job: equally important is allowing them to feel liberated when they come to work, to be creative, to think outside the lines. To foster problem solving and cooperation, for example, we have the Walk a Mile program, in which any employee can do somebody else's job for a day. The operations agents cannot fly the planes, but the pilots can – and do – work as operations agents. (They also, on their own, have held barbecues for all our mechanics, to thank them for keeping our planes flying.) Seventy-five percent of our 20,000 people have participated in the job-swapping program. It's an administrative nightmare, but one of the best tools I know for building understanding and collaboration.

Training is another way you forge committed partnerships. Naturally an airline must train every employee, but our most important training is not in how to manage or administer but in how to lead. Originally that training was part of our pilots' crew-resource management program; it focused on how the first officer and the pilot relate to each other, how they exchange information, and how they focus on the task at hand. In short, how they work as a team. Today we have reservation sales agents, flight attendants, mechanics, administrative staff in those classes, as well as the cockpit crews.

He has realised that everyone in the company is a salesperson to some extent. It's just as important for the company receptionist to be clued into the business code as it is the top salesman or woman, or the most senior executive.

Michael Burkhardt, Southwest Airlines' recruiter, frames the company policy like this in an article in *Business* magazine in April 2006:

> When a team is working well, there is a synergy, and it's
> a joy to come to work. The best organizations know the
> importance of getting the right players on their team. What
> can you do to capitalize on your whole team's observations
> and input in hiring associates who will fit and even
> enhance your culture? The cost of a poor hire is too high.

The cost he's talking about is not only financial, although that can be humbling. (Consider the bill from the recruiting agency, the expense of advertising, the hourly bill for your time.) It's the detrimental effect the wrong candidate can wreak on a cooperating team that really counts, so it's vital to attract the appropriate personalities on to your staff. In fact, some tigers will go so far as to hire the right people even when there are no obvious openings in the company – and then create a job for them. This underlines the high value they place on employing top-quality staff.

I have often come across companies that spend more on equipment than on the people they hire. The old adage 'You get what you pay for' rings true in all things, but especially when it comes to employment.

The next step is to get the right staff in the right positions. Often in organisations, I come across an exceptional individual who is not happy in what they are doing or struggling to succeed, no matter how hard they try. Moving them to a different career within the organisation has produced wonderful results. They were already tigers, but they were placed in the lions' den, where they felt uncomfortable.

A friend of mine, Stuart Thompson, used to run one of the most successful financial services companies in Dubai. He has since retired to develop golf courses. Stuart was a master recruiter and tended towards one of two responses when confronted by candidates after the interviewing process. Sometimes he said, 'I have listened to everything you have to say and examined your curriculum vitae. Everything in front of me says you will be able to do the job. Yet I have a gut feeling that says no. On this occasion you have been unlucky.'

Alternatively, he may have said, 'You have shortcomings in particular areas. You didn't interview that well and your CV has holes in it. But I have seen something about you that I like. I think we can mould you into the person we want.'

This is a guy who was prescriptive about the job and he outlined what was expected before anyone signed on the dotted line. The day begins at 8 a.m. sharp and for two hours employees are expected to deal with paperwork, emails and client enquiries. At 10.30 there's a sales meeting and between 11 a.m. and 5 p.m. staff members are expected to see clients. After that they are due back in the office to make notes about the day.

Among the perks of the job is membership of two organisations of the candidate's choice, anything from a golf club to the local Round Table. Time is set aside for two meetings each month linked to these organisations.

There's an office dress code of dark suits, light shirts and conservative ties. Everyone is expected to attend training courses and Stuart is likely to be shadowing them for three months. About 30 per cent of people hear him out during the interview, then reject the job opportunity, saying the conditions are too restrictive. But those who stay are mentally prepared for the challenge. They've bought into the concept before they start and most are contented and successful in the post.

The Hero Inside

People have hidden depths, extraordinary energies that can be tapped in the right circumstances by people who take the time to do so.

Take Dick Hoyt, for example, a regular guy who has carried out amazing feats – astonishing even himself. Eighty-five times he's pushed his disabled son, Rick, more than 26 miles in marathons. Eight times he's not only pushed him 26 miles in a wheelchair but also towed him 2.4 miles in a dinghy while swimming, and pedalled him 112 miles in a seat on the handlebars – all in the same day.

Dick has also pulled him in cross-country skiing and taken him on his back mountain climbing. And what has Rick done for his father? Strange as it sounds, it's likely that he saved Dick's life.

The story began in Winchester, Massachusetts, more than 40 years ago, when Rick was strangled by the umbilical cord during birth, leaving him brain-damaged and unable to control his limbs.

'He'll be a vegetable the rest of his life,' doctors told Dick and his wife, Judy, when Rick was nine months old. They advised the couple to seek residential care for their son.

But the Hoyts weren't convinced. They noticed the way Rick's eyes followed them around the room and suspected that inside he was just like every other child.

When Rick was 11 they took him to the engineering department at Tufts University and asked if there was anything to help the boy communicate. University staff were doubtful – until Rick laughed at a joke.

In fact his brain was pin-sharp and communication was the real problem. Rigged up with a computer that allowed him to control the cursor by touching a switch with the side of his head, Rick was finally able to converse, albeit silently. His first words were not 'Hi, dad', as Dick might have hoped, but rather a reflection of his support for a Boston ice-hockey team. He said, 'Go Bruins!'

After a high school classmate was paralysed in an accident and the school organised a charity run for him, Rick typed out, 'Dad, I want to do that.'

But how was Dick – middle-aged and out of condition – going to push his son for five miles? Unable to resist the challenge, he tried. 'Then it was me who was handicapped,' Dick says. 'I was sore for two weeks.'

That day changed Rick's life. 'Dad,' he typed, 'when we were running, it felt like I wasn't disabled any more!'

And that single sentence was sufficient to transform Dick's life. He became obsessed with giving Rick that liberated feeling as often as he could. He got into such great shape that he and Rick were ready to try the 1979 Boston Marathon. Initially he was denied the opportunity by a race official. The Hoyts weren't quite a single runner, nor were they a wheelchair entry. For a few years Dick and Rick just joined the massive field and ran anyway until they found a copper-bottomed way to get into the race officially. In 1983 they ran another marathon so fast they made the qualifying time for Boston the following year.

Then somebody suggested a triathlon, which adds cycling and swimming to the mix.

Once again it seemed unlikely that a man who had never learned to swim and hadn't ridden a bike since childhood was going to haul a 50-kilo (110-pound) co-competitor through a triathlon. Still, Dick tried – and felt some considerable achievement in doing so.

Now they've done 212 triathlons, including four gruelling 15-hour Ironman competitions in Hawaii.

Dick has no desire to be a lone competitor. He does it purely for 'the awesome feeling' he gets seeing Rick with a cantaloupe smile as they run, swim and ride together.

At ages 65 and 43, Dick and Rick finished their 24th Boston Marathon, in 5,083rd place out of more than 20,000 starters. Their best time? Two hours, 40 minutes in 1992 – only 35 minutes off the world record, which is held by a regular runner.

'No question about it,' Rick types. 'My dad is the Father of the Century.'

So how did Rick come to save his father's life? Two years ago he had a mild heart attack and discovered his arteries were 95 per cent clogged. 'If you hadn't been in such great shape,' one doctor told him, 'you probably would've died fifteen years ago.' So, in a way, Dick and Rick kept each other alive.

Dick says about his son, 'He inspired me. To me he is the one out there competing. I'm just bringing my arms and legs along. There is something that gets to me when I'm with Rick in competitions that means we are able to go faster.'

Rick says, 'I may be disabled but I live a very fulfilling life and if someone takes the time to get to know me they will realise I'm no different from anyone else.'

Rick, who has his own apartment (he gets home care) and works in Boston, and Dick, retired from the military and living in Holland, Massachusetts, bring out the best in each other. In short, it's the sort of relationship that employers and employees should be looking for. Everyone has a hero inside. Showing just a little above-the-norm behaviour can make the day swing.

Accentuate the Positive

We've looked at whom you might want to work alongside. Now here's a peep at those you don't. For just as some people are uplifting, illuminating and energising, others are disconsolate, dreary and depressive.

I'm sure you've encountered negative people on a daily basis, since there are scores of them about. Without exception, these downbeats are underachievers who are intensely jealous of tigers while finding every excuse as to why they are not conquering goals themselves.

Negative types are lazy and their closed minds exclude new and potentially profitable ideas for the sole motivation of earning money. That means they will put the interests of a client below their own.

Fans of J.K. Rowling's *Harry Potter* books will know them better as Dementors (soul-sucking, wraith-like creatures that feed on the positive emotions of humans). Being drained of life by the presence of negative people is a horrifyingly common experience. They are like a huge dark cloud that descends and saps every ounce of energy from you.

Optimists are far more successful, more healthy and enjoy better relationships than people who view the world negatively. But often they are in the minority. I love to be around positive, motivated people. They say success rubs off but, in my experience, so does negativity. I have been taught two Arabic phrases by a friend from the United Arab Emirates, which have relevance here.

The first is, 'Tell me who you go with and I will tell you who you are.' This means you can tell a lot about a person by the company they keep. The other is, 'If you travel with others for 40 days you will become one of them.' This is a clever comment on the influence other people can have over you.

Is there anyone in your organisation who tries to knock you off your perch every time you talk about a big idea? Steer clear, or they will drag you down to their low level. In both the short and long terms, it's far better to mix with positive, enthusiastic and happy people.

When I first came to the UK one of the sales representatives who regularly called was a thoroughly miserable guy whom, frankly, I found exhausting. If I knew he was on his way I would go and hide in the toilet. But he would bang on the door until I emerged.

'Hey, how are you doing? How is this great life treating you?' I would say. With drooping shoulders and a furrowed brow he'd reply, 'Bearing up under the strain.'

I used to feel sorry for him and give him some business. But I often wondered if he left saying to himself, 'Another sucker caught today.' He didn't last long before going off to pastures new. If he had modified his attitude just a little he could have been more successful and genuinely happier.

It's more difficult to maintain a positive mental attitude than to be miserable, so anyone who makes the effort is likely to be a better business bet because they will put in additional effort and go the extra mile. Identify these people swiftly, because they will help you reach and achieve your goals.

By the same token, you have a responsibility to maintain a positive outlook, even on days when you feel down. This is especially true if you are heading up a team. Those people are looking to you to lead by example, so don't cross the line into negative ground. I know I have driven around car parks giving myself a severe talking to and smiling like a lunatic into the vanity mirror just to get myself into the right frame of mind for office life. Letting standards as fundamental as a positive mental attitude slip will surely have a swift effect on the balance sheet.

Eliminate the Negative

Working with different organisations around the world, I have discovered that the top 20 per cent in business are tigers and they just keep achieving, whatever the circumstances. Next come the 60 per cent of *potential* tigers who haven't yet made the grade – what I call the 'steady Eddies'. They are loyal, hard-working and the lifeblood of most businesses, although they seldom receive the recognition they deserve. Then come the bottom 20 per cent, who are the people who should have been fired ages ago. This is the niche of those with a negative mental attitude. They do just enough to keep their job, but rarely contribute anything positive to the organisation.

As an employer, you are always thinking that you should give these people a second chance or that someday they will come good. The hardest and smartest decision you will ever make is to replace those who are a negative influence on everyone they encounter. All the good work that comes out of a lively, vibrant meeting is soon undone if afterwards a few grim-faced people start exerting a malign influence on everyone else, bad-mouthing new ideas and rubbishing personnel. At the very least the negative influences will demotivate fellow staff members, infecting them like a contagious disease.

I'm part of an organisation called the Professional Speakers Association and some years back five of us formed a committee to organise the following year's conference. The first thing we needed was a venue and someone recommended a hotel in Birmingham. We decided to hold our first meeting there to assess the place.

We sat down and wanted to order some coffee but when we looked towards the bar we noticed two members of staff who were apparently graduates of a training programme that taught them that, if they did not make eye contact with customers, they did not need to serve them. Eventually one of them sauntered over to me and began proceedings with a short, hostile, 'What?'

We ordered coffee, already feeling that this might not be the right venue for our conference. All of us were smartly dressed but when we wanted to order lunch the same waiter said to me, 'I want you to pay cash. Last week some people came in here dressed smartly like you and didn't pay.'

As you might imagine, we chose not to have our conference there. I just wonder how much revenue that hotel is losing because of its negative staff.

The problem surely lies with the hotel management. Managers are probably paying minimum wages, provide no training or motivation and do not monitor what is happening.

Tardy waiters are the hospitality industry's equivalent of lazy receptionists. Businesses create the right impression when the telephone is answered within three rings. If it rings out, then prospective customers soon feel like shopping elsewhere.

Then there are lax shop assistants. Recently I wanted to buy a fax machine and went to a well-known chain store in search of the best deal. 'What's the difference between these two machines?' I asked a young man who was serving customers. After looking at both machines, he turned to me and said, 'Twenty pounds.' I could hardly believe my eyes when he then began reading the descriptions from the boxes to give me an answer. Soon I scurried out of there and went to a small, family-run business in the high street. The staff knew the shop's products inside out and couldn't do enough to help. Needless to say, that's where I placed my business. If it cost a few more pounds it was well worth the expense.

Don't forget that satisfied customers become powerful free

advertising agents. They will tell at least a handful of people about their good experiences at the hands of your company. Those who are treated badly tend to broadcast the fact to at least twice as many and are prone to exaggeration as well.

Is there anyone who is negative in your organisation that may be affecting business, results and morale? How do you motivate yourself to stay positive each day?

A positive mental attitude is, in essence, the result of confidence and enthusiasm. You're sure of yourself, you give the impression that what you're marketing is the best product of its type and you're working for an excellent company. If you're a manager you owe it to your staff and your business to inflate that sense of self-confidence among those on your team.

Did you know that being miserable is a habit – and so is being happy? The choice is yours. Realise as well that everybody faces rejection and failure. Successful people just learn how to handle and control the rejection. You know they see failure as a learning experience, the opportunity of developing new skills and a path back to success.

Here are some of the things I have learned from the tigers regarding finding the right people.

- **Know what you're looking for**

  You must detail the exact profile of the person you want for the position. Be very specific with regard to attitude, dress and propriety, technical ability, skills, past success patterns and everything else that you feel is necessary for that position. Only by really knowing what you want can you start to find the person who naturally fills the position. Take as much time and as many interviews as necessary – this is one of the most expensive investments your business makes. It will cost you in recruitment fees and in training and management time, and, most importantly, it will affect the relationships with your existing clients if you get it wrong.

- **Have a track to follow**
Develop a questionnaire that will accurately evaluate the prospective recruit and give reasons why they should join your organisation. I use a four-page questionnaire that paints an accurate picture of the recruit and helps to evaluate whether he or she is the right person for the organisation.

- **Use an impartial, proven recruitment tool**
I use a computer program called Sales Success Profile. The recruit completes a questionnaire. The answers to 50 questions are fed into a computer, which produces a seven-page report. This highlights the strengths and weaknesses in 13 selling skills. Important areas highlighted are, for example, whether the person is ethical, has enthusiasm, is trainable, is burned out, etc. This is also an excellent tool that highlights weaknesses and areas to be concentrated on when the person joins.

- **Listen to your gut instinct**
If the person looks fantastic on paper and sells themselves well, but your gut instinct leaves you feeling uncomfortable, don't hire – nine times out of ten you will be right.

- **Choose a professional venue**
Use the best hotel or venue available – first impressions count. One of the most professional organisations that I work with uses the Dorchester Hotel, one of the most prestigious in London, and consequently it attracts quality recruits.

- **Make expectations clear**

  Let the recruit know exactly what they can expect from you
  and let them also know exactly what you expect from them.

- **Detail the specifics of the job**

  This may seem trivial, but is often overlooked. Let them
  know what they will be expected to do, detail the working
  hours and what time you expect them to be in the office
  each day. Tell them about the dress code, activity levels and
  any other pertinent details. Get them to agree to all the
  points.

- **Sell with passion**

  If the person is good, they buy you. I have worked with some
  people who are extremely boring and waffle endlessly, and
  any strong recruit will immediately dismiss this company and
  look for a leader with enthusiasm. Remember, in their minds
  they're saying, 'Would I like to work with this person?'

- **Follow up swiftly**

  If you like the person and offer them the position, complete
  contracts immediately. Recruits are impressed and, once they
  have signed the contracts, they are committed. After they
  have sold the position, though, many recruiters then hand
  the process over to an administrative body that may not
  have been properly trained, doesn't know how to deal with
  new recruits and won't realise the urgency of the follow-up.
  In my experience, this is the stage where the entire process
  comes unstuck. It's just like selling: if we leave the client for
  too long, they lose their passion to buy, or they buy from
  someone else. The first three months for any new employee
  is the most crucial period; how you train, mentor, coach and

encourage them during this period will establish their future success with your organisation.

- **Keep your promises**
Follow up everything that you have promised with a letter. Meet prospective candidates at the office, welcome them, help them by joint calling (that is, accompanying them on a call) and do everything in your power to help them to succeed. If you don't, all the time and money you've invested in recruiting the person is in vain. High staff turnover and low morale follow.

Avoid the Pitfalls

Here are some common recruiting errors:

- not asking tough questions;

- overselling the company;

- asking for information you already have;

- allowing interruptions;

- talking too much;

- not detailing the exact requirements of the position;

- setting time limits for the interview;

- hiring in a hurry.

Adversity reveals genius.
HORACE

Watch, listen, and learn. You can't know it all yourself. Anyone
who thinks they do is destined for mediocrity.
DONALD TRUMP

Let our advance worrying become advance thinking and
planning.
WINSTON CHURCHILL

Whether you think you can or think you can't – you're right.
HENRY FORD

The only place where success comes before work is in the
dictionary.
VIDAL SASSOON

Always do right. This will gratify some people and astonish
the rest.
MARK TWAIN

Chapter 5

Good Habits

As he soared in space, the sight of Earth suspended in a rich velvet universe left space shuttle commander Richard Searfoss in wonder. He is one of a privileged few to have seen the planet at such a distance and the incredible view made a big impact.

'It's so sublime,' he told me. 'Every part of the world looks different and the scene is constantly changing. Even if you pass over the same region twice it has different weather conditions or light. It never gets boring looking at Earth out of the window of a spacecraft.'

Although he loved the feeling of weightlessness – 'the sensation of floating in outer space is just phenomenal' – it was the vision of the sedately spinning globe that left the biggest impression.

Being part of shuttle missions was hard work that he likens to long and arduous sprint races. Nevertheless, he still found time for the odd gravity-free somersault as he went about his space-bound business. 'There are no rules that say you can't have fun while you work.'

It is from his life as an astronaut that Richard learned lessons that would hold him in good stead in the business world.

Like many boys, Richard dreamed of being an astronaut from an early age. Perhaps he had a special insight as his dad was a military aircraft pilot. Indeed, Richard himself did a spell as a jet fighter pilot before moving to the NASA programme.

Still, his chances of success were always slim. NASA recruited its astronaut classes about every two years and out of about 3,000 applicants only 20 would be successful.

'I had my disappointments but I've always been focused and a hard worker and I zeroed in on things I saw as goals,' he explained. Yet it is not his against-all-odds success that has shaped his approach to the business world in which he now works as a motivational speaker. Although he underlines the similarities between outer-space flight and business top flight – in that both require superior preparation, leadership and teamwork – he has another essential attribute in mind when it comes to success.

Heading his priority list in leadership qualities is trustworthiness. 'This is a first-order requirement in any effective organisation,' he declared. 'Always be a stand-up person if you want to succeed.'

Of course, it is not the only tenet he lives by. Perhaps not surprisingly, given his background, he chooses passages from a John F. Kennedy speech made on 12 September 1962 about space exploration to reinforce his message to business people.

'We choose to go to the moon in this decade and do ... things, not because they are easy, but because they are hard, because that goal will serve to organise and measure the best of our energies and skills, because that challenge is one that we are willing to accept, one we are unwilling to postpone, and one which we intend to win ...'

Richard paraphrases it thus: 'Set the bar high.' He believes a team is like a matrix, with those in it connected by different and various relationships. With sound leadership, he says, the relationships are duly improved and the team works at its optimum best.

Another role of a leader, he believes, is to break down the barriers that hinder communication. It means constantly monitoring feedback and being as open as possible.

His first space outing was as pilot aboard the space shuttle *Columbia* in 1993. Three years later he was pilot aboard the space shuttle *Atlantis* and was instrumental in its docking with the Russian space station Mir.

In 1998 he was back aboard *Columbia*, this time as mission commander, helping to steer it towards its total of 300 days in space and more than 4,800 earth orbits. After clocking up 39 days in space, Richard retired from the air force with the rank of colonel and left NASA.

Five years later *Columbia* disintegrated 40 miles above Texas as it re-entered the atmosphere at 18 times the speed of sound, killing the seven astronauts aboard.

An astronaut cannot fail to come away from NASA without an acronym, he jokes. His is PAPA, which stands for *preparation*, *awareness*, *persistence* and *accountability*. It is with these words that cutting-edge scientific exploration intersects with the business community as both seek out-of-this-world results.

For Richard, integrity has been at the heart of everything he has done, although other good habits garnered from his experiences in space travel have been switched to a business setting. There's plenty we can borrow from the experiences of people like him to secure our place at the top in the commercial world today.

The Habits of Top Performers

Top salespeople know the difference between being busy and being effective. It means learning the art of delegating. Often this is a skill that doesn't come naturally, so here are a few pointers to help you along the way.

Teach your staff to think and work as you do – but don't be a perfectionist. If they've carried out a task to the best of their ability, then great; the fact that you would have done it differently or better becomes irrelevant after it's been delegated. After all, you've invested that time on other responsibilities, which is how it should be. One tiger I spoke to revealed, 'I empower my support team to take complete responsibility.' Isn't that fantastic?

Remember, the tigers are producing, say, a million pounds' worth of business each year, yet they have the same amount of time each day as the rest of us. They simply work 100 per cent more effectively and part of that talent comes from a mastery of delegation. One memorable approach from a tiger is this: 'I only do what I can do best and delegate the rest. I do not attempt to be all things to all people.'

I often see people in organisations working incredibly long hours and seeming to get very little done. They waste all their time on shuffling papers, pointless emails and other things that may be fun to do but are not effective. There are plenty of good habits to get into that will help sidestep that elephant trap.

Learn to love your Dictaphone or digital recorder. After each telephone call or business meeting, commit your thoughts to tape while they are fresh in your mind.

Start speed-reading, since today we are inundated with paperwork, magazines, newspapers and so forth. It's important not to miss pertinent pieces, so scan them all and tear out interesting items. Set aside time in your week to catch up with reading, ideally while travelling on the train or awaiting an appointment.

Teach yourself to touch each piece of paper that comes across your desk only once. So always remember the three Ds: *delegate* it, *destroy* it or *do* something about it.

Early in my career I used to sit at a desk covered in small individual notes, easy to overlook and easily lost. A tiger I know (my wife) suggested I have a thick notepad on my desk to jot down calls and conversations. I dated them and then always had an essential resource at my fingertips. This has meant I am much more effective and organised.

Don't forget, you don't get a second chance to make a first impression. It's important to be well turned out and well prepared, for both interviews and client meetings.

Tigers realise the importance of clear communication. While their knowledge and skills are impeccable, when it comes to a selling situation, they are straightforward and easy to understand. This was brought home to me many years ago when I was watching a tape of Mehdi Fakharzadeh, who was an Iranian who went to work in America. He soon became one of the top producers in his field and has been the subject of many books and films. On video he told a story about how he tackled an extremely complex business insurance proposal with a team of solicitors. Other financial advisers who had been in before him gave the lawyers 50-page proposals, which the recipients had spent hours, days and weeks trawling through. At the end of it all, these potential clients were still baffled. Mehdi's proposal was short and sweet, and after they had read it, these lawyers said to him, 'You know, all of these other chaps have given us huge proposals and we couldn't understand them. Yours is so concise, we understand it perfectly. How did you manage to keep it so simple?' Mehdi's reply was, 'I'm Iranian, I don't know enough English to make it difficult.'

And isn't that true? Sometimes we as salespeople can complicate business matters so much that we deter the clients. So, when customers say, 'I'll think about it', they really mean, 'I haven't a clue what you're talking about.' So start every process with a KISS, which means 'Keep it simple, stupid.'

Time Management

I know many business people who are disorganised in their daily schedules. To them I would say go on a time-management course and listen carefully to what's said. If it overhauls a haphazard approach then it's worth the investment of time and money tenfold.

Coaching time management is an art in itself. But here's a list of indicators that might help you make some incremental changes that have a big impact in the long term.

Time-management check list

1. Do I wake up too late in the morning?

2. Am I up too late at night?

3. Do I read the newspaper in the morning for too long?

4. Do I linger at home or at the office?

5. Do I work by appointment?

---

6. Do I use waiting time to read, write or think about things related to my business?

7. Do I use non-selling hours, such as evenings and weekends, to best advantage?

8. Does my daily plan say what I'll do next, or do I make it up as I go along?

9. Could someone else do those personal chores for me to make me more productive?

10. Do I prioritise activities so that I do the most important things first?

Early Birds

Most tigers I've worked with have the ability to be fresh and motivated very early in the morning, knowing this will be one of their most productive times of day.

Without telephone calls and numerous other interruptions they can achieve as much in the first two hours of their working day as most people achieve in the subsequent eight. So one small change that can make a significant difference is to get up an hour earlier each day.

Tigers also realise the importance of having full diaries, but this leaves no time for paperwork between the hours of nine and five. By starting the day an hour earlier they can plough through administrative duties unhindered before concentrating wholly on clients.

On the subject of appointments, most tigers have a weekly minimum of 15, or three a day. One piece of wisdom I picked up from a tiger was to make Mondays especially busy. 'If you have a great Monday it's impossible to have a bad week.'

When I first joined the company in London I was fortunate enough to watch an effective early-bird businessman in action. He would arrive at the office at 6.30 and sit with his personal assistant for two hours going through files, discussing business and either doing something about business or delegating it to his PA. If sales representatives wanted to see him, this was the time. He had the uncanny knack of being able to deal with his PA and listen to the sales representative at the same time (which was extremely unnerving for the poor rep). From 8.30 a.m. to 5.30 p.m. was client time, and then he would return to the office, sit with his PA for another hour going through the day's business before going home.

Ten Rules for the Good Life

Taken from 'A Decalogue of Canons for Observation in Practical Life', written in 1825 by Thomas Jefferson.

1. Never put off till tomorrow what you can do today.

2. Never trouble another for what you can do yourself.

3. Never spend your money before you have it.

4. Never buy what you do not want because it is cheap; it will never be dear to you.

5. Pride costs us more than hunger, thirst, and cold.

6. Never repent of having eaten too little.

7. Nothing is troublesome that we do willingly.

8. Don't let the evils which have never happened cost you pain.

9. Always take things by their smooth handle.

10. When angry, count to ten before you speak; if very angry, count to one hundred.

Can't Stop, Won't Stop

It is all about persevering, picking up the phone, making that call, doing the things that you normally don't like to do. You see, the tigers persevere where others give up, as successful people have the habit of doing what the others don't or won't.

I was fortunate enough to speak on the same stage as Iranian Mehdi Fakharzadeh. At 86 years of age (as I write this), he works for just four months a year and has for the last 40 years been the top producer with Metropolitan Life in the USA.

When I interviewed him, I asked him what it was that made him such a success, putting him right up there with the top tigers. He told me that his three principles for success are: hard work, desire and ambition. When I questioned his energy and health he told me that, although he had lived in the US for 58 years, he had never drunk coffee or fizzy drinks or sampled the dubious delights of French fries. Not only does he watch his diet but he also works out frequently. Although he is an incredibly wealthy and successful man, he is very humble and told me that he still has to reach his biggest goal. This is to write $500 million worth of business in one year, an impossible task for anyone except Mehdi.

Tigers have an immense capacity for hard work; their physical stamina is awesome; their ability to persist in their efforts in spite of hardship, loss and opposition defines what they are. For some it starts with just one step at a time. Alvin Law was one of thousands of babies affected by the thalidomide drug during the early 1960s. After he was born with no arms, he was given up for adoption and grew up with far-sighted and determined parents who ensured he made the most of every opportunity that came his way. His talent for music was spotted during school – he plays piano and drums using his toes – and he had a career in broadcasting before becoming a motivational speaker. He has also raised thousands of pounds for charitable causes.

He spells out the qualities needed for today's hard-edged business world using the letters from his name: *attitude*, *learning*, *value*, *imagination* and finally the message, 'Never give up.'

'One of the secrets of life is that you just take it one step at a time and you never, ever know where you just may end up,' he confided.

Think about the artist Vincent van Gogh. When he couldn't afford brushes, he painted without them. Louis Pasteur worked steadily on his ground-breaking vaccines even when his three daughters died. Thomas Edison went week after week without a full night's rest, taking catnaps under his desk as he laboured to perfect the production of electric light. Michelangelo painted the spectacular scenes that have made the Sistine Chapel world-famous with excruciating backache and paint dripping into his eyes, skipping meals and sleep and not even taking the time to change his clothes, so that when he finally removed his socks his skin peeled off with them. This dedication and persistence through circumstances that would dishearten most people is the result of passion and single-mindedness alongside a deep personal conviction.

Guidelines to successful time management

- Establish specific goals in writing.

- Make a daily to-do list and prioritise it.

- Focus on goals, not activities.

- Don't procrastinate.

- Ensure that daily actions relate to your goals.

- Have a quiet time.

- Be decisive.

- Tackle difficult tasks first.

- Keep meetings short.

- Control the telephone – limit and screen calls.

- Do things right the first time.

- Be a good listener.

- Learn to speed-read.

- Improve your writing skills.

- Avoid clutter.

- File neatly.

- Jot everything down in a notebook.

- Plan for tomorrow today.

- Resist idle chatter.

- Delegate the routine.

- Divide major tasks into manageable sections.

- Handle paperwork once only.

- Make time management a daily habit.

You can't change the direction of the wind but you can adjust your sails.
JOHNATHAN SWIFT

A business has to be involving, it has to be fun, and it has to exercise your creative instincts.
RICHARD BRANSON

We don't need more strength or ability or greater opportunity. What we need is to use what we have.
BASIL S. WALSH

It's not the critic who counts, nor the man who points out how the strong man stumbled or where the doer of deeds could have done better. The credit belongs to the man who is actually in the arena, whose face is marred by dust and sweat and blood, who strives valiantly, who errs, comes short again and again, who knows the great enthusiasms, the great devotions and spends himself in a worthy cause, who at the least knows in the end the triumph of high achievement and who at the worst if he fails at least fails while doing greatly so that his place shall never be with those cold and timid souls who know neither victory nor defeat.
THEODORE ROOSEVELT

The price of greatness is responsibility.
WINSTON CHURCHILL

Chapter 6

Think Creatively, Work Smarter

Tigers are creative thinkers who operate outside the box so that they can work smarter rather than harder. Sometimes the word *creative* is associated only with people in the arts. We tend to think of it in terms of painting, writing books and composing. Yet creativity exists in any career or field.

What is creativity? It is really all about being flexible, being imaginative and having the ability to work around any problem, to find fresh solutions, to experiment with new approaches and devise some original plans.

Being creative means that tigers also know when to modify or even jettison any ideas that they have. It makes me think of Henry Ford, who did this with both the automobile itself and the assembly line that ultimately revolutionised car production. A lot of ideas had been explored before his, but he borrowed some and perfected them.

To think creatively, you also have to have a natural curiosity, and this is something that stands out with top people as well. Every tiger has a burning desire to learn. They are always curious, asking questions and looking for answers.

To find the information they seek, they'll study books and publications, confer with experts, travel all over, spend late nights reading and studying and even experimenting, in search of new ideas. This curiosity often leads to wonderful inspiration, which enables them to be productive and prolific. I'm perpetually astonished by the creativity that I see channelled into businesses.

A number of years ago I was asked to do some training for a financial services company in Hong Kong. The owner invited me to come in beforehand to learn about the company and its culture.

I was asked to wait at a metro station, where I was collected by a smartly dressed man driving a luxury car. When we arrived at the offices in a converted house I walked through the gates into a beautiful garden complete with tinkling streams and peaceful music. The company slogan was written on the wall, 'Live a life you love'.

A receptionist took away my mobile phone and asked me what I wanted to drink. The menu she gave me offered every refreshment I could imagine. Now I began to think I was in one of the world's top hotels.

I was then given a tour of this incredible place. 'All our carpets are made of recycled materials,' said one of the receptionists, who was acting as my tour guide. 'The paint we use is environmentally friendly.' Consideration had gone into every detail of the building.

I was impressed, not least with these techniques with which the company 'warmed up' its clients. Back in the magical garden I met finally the chief executive officer. I asked her about her sales consultants and the products they sold. They were counsellors, she corrected me, and they were briefed to improve the lives of wealthy Chinese business people rather than sell, sell, sell. Customers were collected from their offices – so the threat of constant interruptions was eliminated – in smart cars and brought to this tranquil oasis. Like mine, their mobile phones were taken from them and they were given drinks and a tour. Afterwards a counsellor spoke to them about finding the right solutions for their business and personal lives. As for the counsellors, they are given a free breakfast daily and treated with dignity – and, it was no surprise to discover, staff turnover was almost non-existent.

Just like the clients, I was treated to a gourmet lunch and I learned that the company hires one of the best chefs available so that meal times are special culinary experiences. At weekends, the premises are hired out to clients for parties and weddings. Typically, their guests are fellow millionaires who are duly impressed with the food, the drink and the aura given off by the place. Monday mornings are punctuated by phone calls with enquiries from these guests. What a creative way to run a business!

The Royal Treatment

Recently I went on holiday to Dubai with my wife. Neither of us is keen on hotel food so we tend to book on a bed-and-breakfast basis, budgeting for evening meals in our spending money.

When we arrived at Le Royal Méridien hotel the receptionist had a surprise in store. One of the eight restaurants attached to the hotel had been voted the best in the United Arab Emirates and to mark the occasion she offered us free evening meals in any of the restaurants for the duration of our stay.

Of course, we were delighted just to have *one* free meal in an award-winning restaurant, let alone a week's worth, but we were still concerned that the food in the other restaurants might not be to our tastes. So on the first night we asked our waiter what the other eateries were like. This man was a skilled salesman. He waxed lyrical about the high standards and the delicious food that was available to us in all the hotel restaurants. Before the evening was over we had planned our meals for the holiday, all of which would be in the hotel.

It was clever salesmanship, for the money we had set aside for eating we willingly spent on aperitifs, fine wines and other treats. And it is of course through drink and not food that hotels make the greatest profits.

Sitting by the pool the following day, I couldn't resist telling a fellow guest of our good fortune. I discovered that he too was eating free of charge in the hotel. It was a clever and creative offer that kept us guests as happy captives.

I then realised the simple appeal of a system rooted in under-promising and overdelivering. The hotel managers knew that most guests would be drawn into Dubai for supper, leaving their restaurants empty. So they came up with an action plan, worked the cost of the suppers into the price of the stay – and left every-one feeling that they were receiving incredible value.

Food wasn't the only area in which the hotel excelled. At the pool and beach each day we were given small, iced, scented face-cloths and spray bottles to cool off – a delightful detail. Staff soon knew us by our names. We had an incredible 10 days and just be-fore leaving I wanted to meet the tiger who ran the hotel and find out more about the success strategy. Pam Wilby had taken over the management a few years before and turned the hotel into one of the best in the group. You can see Pam's formula in the box.

Pam Wilby's Rules for Success

- Treat everyone as an individual.

- Remember names.

- Provide quality-awareness training.

- Ensure you focus on everyday things in a fun way.

- Put the customer first, task second.

- Get the right structures in place.

- Prefer customer to operational focus.

- Provide great food for staff.

- Ensure staff empowerment.

- Create a buddy system for new entrants.

- Commit to an excellence programme.

- Have weekly complaint audits.

- Ensure team building for staff.

- Use a good-ideas scheme – looked at by the executive team.

- Provide staff newsletters.

- Make sure your Employee of the Year goes to London or Paris.

- Use a mystery guest – this is someone who books in as a regular guest, but is assessing everything about the hotel. The staff don't know who they are, so they're treated the same as all the other guests. They then report back to the management on their experience.

- Organise a *Mastermind*-style quiz competition each year as a fun way of keeping staff on their toes.

- Award company 'Oscars' based on:
  - 50% customer feedback;
  - 30% appraisals;
  - 20% managers votes.

  (This is based on the same concept as the real Oscar awards. One night of the year everyone dresses smartly and attends a gala evening where everyone is recognised for their efforts and 'Oscars' are awarded to the exceptional staff.)

I commented on the facecloths and spray bottles at the pool. The idea came from one of the pool attendants, who witnessed how affecting the heat could be. Pam also told me how she encouraged ideas from the staff, who were always coming up with innovative ways of making the customer experience special. After I told her how all the staff remembered our names she revealed that they were taught to do this as part of a training programme. She knew that customers felt special when they were called by their names.

The Small Stuff

On a recent speaking trip to Asia, I was once again pleasantly surprised by the levels of service that I experienced everywhere that I visited. I travel to Kuala Lumpur a number of times each year and have been fortunate enough to stay in some excellent hotels. On this trip, a friend suggested that I try the new Traders Hotel which is part of the Shangri-La group, but aimed more at business people.

The service, food and room were exceptional, but what impressed me most were the small extra things that were done for the guests. On the day I checked out, I found a handwritten note pushed under my door by the chamberman/cleaner. I found him and he told me that he writes a personal note to everyone on his floor on the checkout day. I was so impressed that he received a nice tip.

Dear Mr Furness, Frank
It is sad to know that you are leaving us tomorrow. Thank you for coming and staying here with us. We hope you enjoyed your visit.

It has been my great pleasure to look after your room. I look forward to welcome you back to Traders Hotel, Kuala Lumpur in the near future.
Wishing you a pleasant trip home and a safe journey home,
Wil (room attendant)

A Different View

At the age of 37, Mark Vlassopoulos had riches that most of us can only dream about. London-born Vlassopoulos was an international jet-setter associated with the creation of some of the most profitable nightclubs on the planet.

Three weeks and one financial crisis later he was £50 million in debt. Far from despairing, he set about building up new businesses building casinos and shopping malls until he topped the fortune he once knew. When it came to losing cash, he told me, it was a case of 'easy come, easy go'.

'You have to have excellent stamina to be an entrepreneur,' he explained. 'You've got to be able to stick with what you're doing. There are no fast fixes. Everyone wants to win the game-show millions with an hour of effort. We all know that doesn't work in the real world. Success takes a lot of hard work and a lot of commitment.'

An expert in luxury lifestyle developments, Vlassopoulos thinks his ability to have a vision and stick with it until it is a reality has been critical to his renaissance. For some tastes, his could be described as the creative choice. He decides on risky ventures with a combination of gut instinct and a shrewd scrutiny of circumstances.

'Some of it is seat-of-your-pants stuff, but if a few dots suddenly connect it's probably worth looking at [a business proposition] more deeply. If a few pieces fit together there may be a deal to be done and a contract to be signed.'

But he cautions about excessive ambition. 'If I stepped into all the deals that came across my desk in a week then I would absolutely not have time to deliver on them all. It's important to manage expectations and be real about the ease and speed of a deal. It is often inevitable that a first deal does not come through, but don't worry: others will.'

He says another key to success is maintaining a sense of humour to defend against the hard knocks. Entrepreneurs of 28 going on 78 make life hard for themselves and everybody else, he warns.

His final pointer is perhaps the easiest to learn and the least used in business today. 'Listen to what others have to say. Everybody wants to give us advice, often about stuff that we really don't think we want to hear.'

However, he believes that somewhere in the outpourings from family, friends and colleagues there may be a golden nugget that adds the necessary extra dimension to a business proposition. 'So I do try to listen to what others have to say.'

His aim to see life from a different perspective was enhanced through an encounter with troubled superstar Michael Jackson.

Vlassopoulos and his colleagues had been pressed by financiers to involve a high-profile celebrity in a Las Vegas development. After some time, Michael Jackson agreed to a meeting, which took place in the early hours of the morning.

'We picked Michael up from the refuse area of a hotel. He never goes through the front door because of the attentions of fans. We were driving back to the offices when we realised we had no gas in the car. Within ten minutes we were pumping gas in Nevada with Michael Jackson wearing a matador's hat and pyjamas.

'Michael just got so excited and asked if he could pump the gas. It was the first time in his life he had been to a gas station and used the pumps. It was like my getting a chance to drive the space shuttle. The joy in his eyes was a treasure to see. It is a very sad story about a very talented man.'

It doesn't matter if a venture is worth 10 dollars or 10 million dollars, a tiger will take the same clear-headed businesslike approach.

Success in All Shapes and Sizes

Creative thinking isn't the preserve of the rich, either. When I was visiting the harbour-side monument, the Gateway to India, I encountered two girls, aged about five and eight, who asked me where I came from. When I said England they replied, 'Buckingham Palace, Manchester

United.' Although I doubt they could read or write they then gave me an astonishing tour with dates, names and descriptions. At the end I pulled out ten rupees as a tip but they stopped me. 'Please don't give us any money,' they cried. 'Our papa, he drinks.' Instead, they beckoned me down a side road towards a street vendor, who gave them each a tin of milk powder. As they ran into the distance he asked me for 600 rupees. Speechlessly, I handed over the cash and made my way back to the hotel.

When I got there I explained to the manager what had happened. He threw back his head and laughed. These were professional beggars, he explained, who would quickly return the milk powder and receive 50 rupees each from the vendor. They knew they could improve substantially on the tip I had planned with a bit of creative thinking. I had to admit that I admired their basic business skills. They found a prospect, developed a rapport with me, used their knowledge, worked with their initiative and kept a positive mental attitude when they must have been subject to rejection many times a day.

Looking the Part

Tigers seek the most prestigious office in the best location and in it they put luxurious furniture. It's not all down to polished wood and thick-pile carpets, though. As I travel the world, I can get a feel for a company immediately I walk into its offices. Some are cold and sterile; some are cluttered and disorganised; others just have the most unbelievable vibrancy. They are warm and welcoming, and there is an air of success. This is normally the result of great leadership, hiring, training, motivation and having fun.

However, it is vital to practise good office hygiene, which means being clean and tidy and emanating a pleasant atmosphere. It's the Route One way to impress existing and potential clients. Also, since it's more cost-effective to have clients coming in for appointments rather than taking to the road to visit them, tigers want a venue in which everyone can be comfortable.

These same tigers drive the smartest cars and choose well-cut clothes. After all, why would anyone invest a million pounds with you if you turn up in an old car, wear a threadbare suit and carry a chewed ball point pen? A fact of life is that successful people like to do business with other successful people.

When I do business in the City of London with some of the top investment companies in the world, the game plan is always the same. When I arrive for my appointment the reception area is clean and plush. The receptionist knows my name, doesn't keep me waiting and ushers me straight through to a boardroom. As you might expect, the boardroom is impressively laid out with refreshments served in fine bone china on the table. Within moments the person I'm seeing comes into the room and is instantly attentive. Who could fail to be impressed?

In Canada and America it is often the same story. When I arrive there's a sign by the door welcoming me to the building. This is a company that's proud of itself and enthusiastic towards others. Seeing my name on the sign makes me feel like a special visitor.

And consider the alternative: going to an office with papers piled high on a desk, being kept waiting for 20 minutes and being served tea from a chipped mug. Given a choice, potential investors are going to go only one way – and that's to the place where calm organisation prevails.

Make Creative Choices

Soon after I started in the insurance business in 1980 I was generating a pile of paperwork that I didn't have time to see to myself. There were about 35 consultants at our branch and only two people in what was then called 'the typing pool'. Sometimes I had to wait for days to get the typing done and I knew this would affect my results, so I asked my manager for more administrative support.

Fortunately, my manager saw me as a businessman rather than a salesman. He told me to hire more support staff myself. When I said I couldn't afford the expense of a dedicated staff member, he pointed out that others were in the same boat. Couldn't I get together with them to share the costs?

That's exactly what happened, and my business output rose, just as I suspected it would. It wasn't too long before I could afford to employ an administrative assistant full time to work just for me. I had the right outlook, a creative approach and achieved an amazing result.

Make creative choices by finding clients who are cost-effective. It takes just as much time and effort to do business with people worth £100 as it does to work with those worth £1 million.

Make Connections

Consider working with other professions or companies that will raise your game into the higher income bracket. An excellent market to harvest is that attached to small or medium businesses. Of course, the typical millionaire is the one who began a small business some years back and, through hard labour, built it up into a sound and profitable venture. Probably driving the same car they did five years ago and living in the same modest neighbourhood, these unobtrusive people populate a largely untapped market. They are known as 'the millionaires next door'.

Review the top 20 per cent of your clients and make them your priority. This is the Pareto principle in action, also known as 'the law of the vital few'. It was named after the Italian economist Vilfredo Pareto (1848–1923), who observed that 80 per cent of Italy's national wealth came from 20 per cent of its population. It's a rule that, give or take a small margin, applies in a surprising number of business areas.

At meetings you will probably find that 80 per cent of decisions emerge from 20 per cent of meeting time. Roughly 80 per cent of your managerial problems and headaches are caused by just 20 per cent of your employees, while 80 per cent of a manager's interruptions come from the same 20 per cent of staff members. It is not unusual for just 20 per cent of a sales force to generate 80 per cent of trade while a disproportionate 80 per cent of customers' complaints are probably linked to just 20 per cent of your projects.

And, if only you could work out which 20 per cent of your advertising portfolio is producing 80 per cent of the campaign's results, then you could save a small fortune!

By the Pareto principle we know that it's the bottom 20 per cent that generates 80 per cent of the hassles, so start concentrating on the upper echelon and treat them better than anyone else. If you are having difficulty discovering the clients you'd prefer to be dealing with, consider using experts in the field.

Introducers and professional connections are people who can furnish you with an endless source of leads. Think of anyone who can provide you with names and numbers and whom you can reward either financially or in a similar fashion (with a gift, say).

Make it a part of your monthly target to meet two potential professional introducers and prepare an excellent presentation about how you can work together and what would be in it for them. If you develop enough professional connections providing you with an endless source of leads, your business will sky-rocket.

When I was working in financial services, I would meet up once a month with a partner from a large accounting firm, a law firm and a commercial insurance brokerage. Each of us would bring five good referrals that we would give to the others. The benefit for each of us was that we left the breakfast meeting with 15 qualified referrals from trusted professionals. We would then phone, meet and develop the relationship with the referrals and business would follow. Think about whom you could meet with each month to develop your network.

Be Seen

How socially mobile are you? When I first came to the UK and worked in insurance I needed to mix with people I wanted to sell to, so I joined a golf club, an exclusive cricket club and a health club. It all cost me money, of course, and I spent plenty of time at all three, you won't be surprised to hear. But with remarkable ease the plan produced the results I hoped for, as I was mixing with clients – who eventually became friends and started referring me to others.

The cricket club had a reputation for being snobbish and I had no idea whether membership would yield results. But then I was asked if I would assist with the coaching of the juniors and I readily agreed. Every Friday evening the parents would come to fetch their sons after practice. We would soon strike up conversation, I would make a friend and the business rolled in.

I had been involved with Toastmasters International for 13 years in South Africa. They are one of the largest non-profit, self-development organisations in the world and many of their members are senior executives and professionals wanting to improve their speaking skills. When I arrived in London, I approached them and asked if I could set up a club in the town where I lived. They agreed and within two months I had 25 people as part of the club who were exactly in the target market that I was working.

My advice to everyone is to become socially mobile and be prepared to do business in all circumstances. You can also get involved in great charity organisations such as Rotary and Lions that do so much good for society and at the same time allow you to meet and develop relationships with people in your target market. Presently I have developed a strong relationship with the Chambers of Commerce and Business Links in my area and have done business with or through them at least six times in the past year.

Remember Martin Young of Meyado, who runs his business with the discipline and vision that he learned in the military? We met him in Chapter 2. He is also an excellent polo player and once a year imports talent from South America to form part of his polo team and then sponsors a tournament in Spain. This is a considerable investment, but allows him to socialise for 10 days with some of the wealthiest people in the world. Few organisations get the opportunity to work this target market. The business his company gains as a result of this tournament each year gives him a worthwhile return on his investment in a memorable way.

Have Fun

Tigers are excellent company. I love being around them. They're always enthusiastic, passionate, exciting and creative. They love what they do and have boundless energy and capacity for hard work, but also play just as hard as they work.

When I ran a sales course for a company in Hong Kong in 2004, their top salesman came in looking a bit the worse for wear. He apologised and explained to me that he'd been out until four that morning with one of his clients. It later emerged that this client was a Fortune 500 company that had thrown a party for a thousand of its staff and close business associates. The entertainment for the evening was Tom Jones, who'd been flown in from Las Vegas. It dawned on me that the top salespeople, these tigers, often socialise in circles far different from the norm.

- Set yourself a target of becoming involved in at least two clubs, charities, self-development organisations.

- Attend meetings at least weekly, network and develop relationships.

- Volunteer to be part of the committee or management. Get into a position of power and help others.

- Arrange monthly meetings with your professional introducers with a view to cross-referencing clients.

- Educate them in very simple terms on what you do and how you can help them.

- Place articles in their newsletters.

- Copy the introducers on all correspondence relating to shared clients.

Some of us are so self-reliant that we won't ask for help from our family members or close friends. You can't do it all, all the time, by yourself.

YASMEEN ABDUR-RAHMAN

A man should never neglect his family for business.

WALT DISNEY

I believe that being successful means having a balance of success stories across the many areas of your life. You can't truly be considered successful in your business life if your home life is in shambles.

ZIG ZIGLAR

It's not enough to make time for your children. There are certain stages in their lives when you have to give them the time when they want it. You can't run your family like a company. It doesn't work.

ANDREW GROVE, FOUNDER OF INTEL

Chapter 7

Balancing Act

All work and no play may makes Jack a dull boy, but, more crucially, it harms your chances of becoming a tiger. Time and again tigers have told me how important it is to attend to the work–life balance. It's an area too often neglected in business by those who mistakenly feel their focus is blurred by anything other than their job.

Work–life balance is more than just human-resources jargon. It is the key to living the good life, and that's why it is so important to tigers. We all know people who work for 16 hours a day, never visit the gym and hardly see their families. They may have plenty of cash but they are far from healthy and happy, so, in my view, these people have missed out on success.

Countless surveys have proved that the necessary equilibrium is absent in most working families. In 2007 the British Social Attitudes report found that eight out of ten men and women working full time wanted to spend more hours with their families. At the same time, men and women feel they are expected to work harder than ever before. The desire to spend more time at home with the family than at work had increased significantly over the previous 18 years (since the survey was last carried out), with no fewer than 84 per cent of full-time women and 82 per cent of full-time men saying that was their aim. A majority of men and women say the demands of their job interfere at least sometimes with family life.

These figures are bad enough but, when you consider that on average Britons spend fewer hours at work each week than Americans, Australians and the Japanese, it's apparent that this is a worldwide issue.

Tigers have cracked the work–life balance issue, if my own survey is anything to go by.

Successful managers need to be emotionally stable to cope with the daily demands of their job. This steadiness comes directly from a happy home life. I discovered that most top business people have strong relationships with their spouses and are close to their children.

Family values, ethics and morals remain as vital as closing a deal, illustrating that having a strong home life doesn't mean forgoing business success. I was struck by one response I received in my survey of tigers which read, 'a loving atmosphere in your home is the foundation for your life'.

Nor will tigers ignore their own physical well-being. Most of them have a regular fitness regime and watch their eating habits in order to harness sufficient energy to achieve their goals.

A further dimension is the importance of spiritual life. When you attend weekend conventions, particularly in America, it is striking how many top achievers attend the optional Sunday sessions for worship.

But another thing that struck me about tigers is how much they give back to the community. So many of them are involved in community projects or charitable work. In fact, one of the top achievers I know personally gives away 30 per cent of his gross income to worthy causes each year. It brings to life the biblical advice to give in order to receive.

Make Time and Take Time

Perhaps this point won't be too popular with those who employ tigers, but it is essential to take sufficient holidays. Nobody has the capacity to work hard all of the time, and, if that's what you rely on to get you to the top, you will burn out at some stage. Colds, fatigue and stress are all symptoms of a scorched-earth policy in business. It's no way to keep a grip on the upper echelons of performance.

A top achiever I know in South Africa takes every eleventh week off. At the beginning of each year he takes his planner and draws a line through that week to ensure he is off the diary. This is when he goes on holiday, spends time with his family, unwinds and recharges. He does this regardless of conventions or business meetings. The habit has become like a religion for him. And for the last 20 years or so he has become one of the top producers not only in his company but also in the insurance industry.

Of course, high-level executives ensure they are ready for any task ahead. Perhaps it goes without saying that they are organised at work with the necessary training and information under their belts, and plenty of preparation goes into each day so they can perform at their best, as previous points in this book have already shown.

But they put just as much effort into their domestic duties. Tigers have their holidays booked, go to their children's concerts or sports matches, attend family functions and also devote time to playing sport, supporting charities and being at community events.

Attention to detail is important here, and it is in this area that our tigers stay ahead of the game. Consider your life at the moment. If there are any areas that demand more organisation, start putting together a plan of action. Ask yourself some challenging questions. How much quality time do you spend with your family? How effective is your exercise routine? Have you stopped doing any of the recreations or pastimes that you once enjoyed? What can you do right now to lead a more balanced life?

If you are a manager, or aspire to be one, it is important also to take time with others on the staff. No matter how high their personal standards are set, some people's performances will dip if they have troubles at home, illness in the family or financial difficulties. Maintain high levels of empathy so you can see a situation from somebody else's point of view. Don't forget, you are probably dealing with someone who has above-average ambition and a sharpened desire to succeed. If these qualities begin to flag, there may be a simple and easily surmountable issue at the root of the problem. For a boss it's important to know when employees need a friendly ear, an arm around their shoulder and a little time investment. They need to attend the school play or sports day just as you do.

Sometimes employees have a crisis of confidence that affects their work. You can help by gently coaxing their self-esteem back to full strength by focusing on their behaviour, monitoring outcomes, reinforcing good results and providing feedback. If their self-doubt is caused by lack of competence, ensure some training is made available. Find out whether their product knowledge is up to scratch, since this could hamper their efforts at work. Exceptional leaders believe indecision is a fatal weakness in underlings and that a weak decision is better than no decision. Write this office policy large and it may soothe away some underlying stress.

Open-Door Policy

Approachability is a golden asset in management so make sure your office door is never shut. Some managers choose to rule by fear and a surprising number of companies operate against a groundswell of quaking and cringing. It does not motivate staff, however, and any results it brings about usually cannot be sustained in the long term. It's always more productive to consider a pat on the back rather than a kick up the backside. The difference may only be a few vertebrae but it's about 100 times more effective.

I'm not talking about being best buddies with people on the payroll. However, the qualities that most employees are questing for in management are sincerity, even handedness, enthusiasm, good counsel and generosity of spirit. Make sure you can tick those boxes in business. Lead by example, always do what you say you will and manage people as individuals. It means looking to yourself first for answers before laying the blame for poor performance or a hostile atmosphere at the door of others. Take the time to mark birthdays, remember the names of spouses and children, organise social events, and the bonds that tie your team together will soon hold fast.

The motivation guru Zig Ziglar tells a story that illustrates just how easy it can be to lose sight of the work–life balance. He recalls an interview with a young man who worked from 6 in the morning until 11 at night, six days a week. So tired was he that he nearly crashed his car on several occasions. His marriage was running into trouble thanks to the amount of time he spent away from home.

Why did he pursue such a demanding routine? Well, his hardworking manager was his hero and he wanted to emulate the guy.

'I asked him whether the manager was happy,' says Zig. 'He replied, "I don't think he is happy at all. I almost never hear him laugh and he seldom smiles. He has ulcers."'

Although the manager had money coming out of his ears, his wife was divorcing him, he had no peace of mind, he was only moderately successful and he had no friends. The young man was swift to add, 'I'm not his friend. I just admire him because he is so successful. To tell you the truth, he is a somewhat of a jerk.'

Zig was able to make the young man see he was looking to the wrong guy for inspiration. As a result he changed his job, fast-tracked up the ladder and had a happy, secure home life once more.

So, for all sorts of reasons, it's vital that managers come up to the mark.

'Me' Time

The most successful people in business are investors – and they're not scared to invest in their most important asset: themselves. Anything that enhances their potential is seen as of top value. Tigers work continually to find the best path to achievement and then put in whatever it takes in order to start down that path. They are constantly reading, investing and listening to tapes and CDs, and they also seek out other people similar to themselves. They mix with them, swap ideas and form *Mastermind* quiz groups.

I attended the Tom Hopkins seminar – an annual event – in 1998, three days of sales training that focuses on getting back to basics. It was quite an intense course, called a boot camp. There were 800 people who had come to the course and I thought that they might be new to sales, but I was wrong! These were some of the giants in the industry, many of them earning more than a million dollars a year. I asked, 'Why are you here when you're earning over a million dollars a year?' And the reply was pretty uniform. 'Whenever I come here I'm mixing with other positive people and I'm learning about the nuts and bolts of the job all over again. I get back to work refreshed, I start selling and everything goes well. Six or eight months down the line, I start veering off course, forgetting about the basics, so coming back here always puts me on track.'

Another observation that I have made is that great leaders run most top sales teams. On a recent trip to the Far East, I was giving two talks a day in one country, flying out to the next country and repeating the same schedule. Towards the end of the second week, I was really tired and a little apprehensive, because the company that I would be working with on the Saturday was one of the top in its sector in the world. It had a small select team of about 10 people with everyone in the company producing at the highest levels. The chief executive of this company is one of the most motivated, enthusiastic and inspiring people I have ever met. When the group arrived for the meeting, everyone was cheerful, happy and positive, and it turned out to be one of the most exciting days of my life. We started the day at nine o'clock and before we could blink it was five thirty in the afternoon and I'm sure we could have continued right through the night. You see, the thing about tigers is that they're always willing to learn. They don't mind investing their time and their money, as long as they can take away one or two ideas that will make them more productive. They're also willing to share ideas on what makes them successful and would always see the positive aspects rather than the negatives.

The Tiger from Kansas City

Recently I was speaking to the Entrepreneurs' Organisation chapter in Kansas City and was collected at my hotel by an extremely successful young woman, Mary Leonida, who had a number of businesses. When Mary started university, she did not have the money to pay her fees, so she borrowed money from the bank and bought a Kentucky Chicken franchise. After classes and at weekends she worked at the takeaway and soon bought her second. She now owns a number of these franchises, a software company and a film studio. The secret of her success? The out-of-hours learning that she undertook.

Think about your own situation. How much are you spending on self-development? Are there any areas that you can improve on, because if you want to walk with the tigers, you have to study them; you have to study what makes them successful and then start doing what they do.

- **Successful managers need to be emotionally stable to cope with the daily demands of their job. This steadiness comes directly from a happy home life.**

- **Nobody has the capacity to work hard all of the time – it is essential to take sufficient holidays.**

- **Ask yourself how much quality time you spend with your family. How effective is your exercise routine? What can you do right now to lead a more balanced life?**

- The top people I know put about 10 per cent of their time and money back into themselves, going on courses and buying reading materials, tapes and anything else that can help to make them more productive.

Everyone has a talent. What is rare is the courage to follow that talent, the dark place where it leads.

ERICA JONG

Success is not final, failure is not fatal: it is the courage to continue that counts.

WINSTON CHURCHILL

Life is either a daring adventure or nothing. Security does not exist in nature, nor do the children of men as a whole experience it. Avoiding danger is no safer in the long run than exposure.

HELEN KELLER

In life and business, there are two cardinal sins. The first is to act precipitously without thought and the second is to not act at all.

CARL ICHAN, INVESTOR AND ENTREPRENEUR

Every day, you'll have opportunities to take chances and to work outside your safety net. Sure, it's a lot easier to stay in your comfort zone – in my case, business suits and real estate – but sometimes you have to take risks. When the risks pay off, that's when you reap the biggest rewards.

DONALD TRUMP

Chapter 8

Getting Down to Business

For tigers no obstacle is insurmountable when it comes to their stated goals. They'll persevere and do whatever they need to make their dreams come true.

The top tigers realise that sales and marketing are the lifeblood of their success and it's important to get these right.

The Sales Cycle

The sales cycle in most businesses covers the following process:

- prospecting;

- telephoning for appointments;

- the first interview/appointment;

- developing rapport and trust;

- analysing needs/the discovery process;

- preparing the correct solution for the client;

- the second and subsequent interviews;

- presenting solutions that meet the clients' needs;

- negotiating;

- overcoming objections;

- closing; and

- service and follow-up.

A successful sales cycle should increase profits, the goal of most businesses. Sometimes we think the key is to increase the number of clients, but the easiest way to increase profits is to use a three-pronged approach.

1. **Increase** the number of clients.

2. **Increase** the number of times your clients buy from you.

3. **Increase** the average amount they spend with you.

The numbers are really interesting. If you:

- increase the number of clients by 10 per cent;

- increase the number of times they buy by 10 per cent; and

- increase their 'average spend' by 10 per cent, your turnover increases by 33.1 per cent.

So even small changes can make enormous differences. Even more interestingly, if you:

- increase the number of clients by 30 per cent;

- increase the number of times they buy by 30 per cent; and

- increase their 'average spend' by 20 per cent,

your turnover increases by 100 per cent.

Breaking the Ice

Whenever we meet someone new, tension levels can be high, so here are some ideas to help put people at their ease.

You've just met with a potential new client and there's anxiety in the air. This is the stage for small talk, during which you can develop rapport and a business relationship. So what do you speak about? Well, think about it. Whom do people like to talk about best? They love to speak about themselves, an area in which they have unchallenged expertise, so this is the direction to go in conversation.

For many years now, I've used the 'past, present and future' conversation formula to do this. I walk into the prospect's office, have a look around and say, 'This is amazing – you've got this great position with a huge company. How did you get started?' Now nobody's asked him that question for years and he is really proud of what he has achieved, so the floodgates open. 'Well, fifteen years ago I started as a clerk and I worked my way up ...' I just keep quiet and listen.

The next question I ask is about the existing situation. 'So, tell

me about your position at the moment. How are things going?'
Normally he'll say, 'Well I've got fifteen people working for me,
we're expanding and opening three or four new branches ...'
Once again, I just keep quiet and listen.

The next question is about the future and with this I learn
more about the potential client than in any other part of the
interview. 'So where do you see yourself and your company in
five or ten years' time?' This is where clients talk from the heart
and what they will say next will give me all kinds of buying sig-
nals. They may say, 'Well, I want to expand and open another
three branches.' So I focus on how I can help. If I were in recruitment, I would know he's going to need new staff. If my business
were computers, he would need new computer systems. Other
requirements could be: property/rental, consumables, telephone
systems, stationery, office furniture, accounting services, legal
advice. By using 'past, present and future' I have made inroads
that take me towards a sale without undue effort. Also remember
that logic makes people think and emotion makes them act, so
focus on the emotion when selling.

Selling is all about relationships. People buy from people
they trust, like and feel comfortable being with. Coming
from South Africa, where military service was compulsory,
I grew up knowing and respecting guns. At one stage in
South Africa, many of the men used to carry guns, so it
was easy to develop rapport. If I met someone and I saw
a slight bulge in the jacket or ankle, I would pull out my
gun and say, '.38 special – stainless-steel barrel.' They
would then pull out their gun and say, '.45 Colt Magnum,
Packmeister handles.' I would reply, 'I use soft-nose bul-

lets that explode on impact.' And they would reply, 'I use hard-nose bullets, can go through a brick wall.'

This usually developed rapport, but what I didn't realise was that what worked in South Africa does not necessarily work anywhere else in the world. I walked in and saw my first overseas client, pulled out my gun and never saw him again.

The Ben Duffy Method

Many years ago I was taught a method of relaxing clients and clearing any roadblocks before they could affect my sale appointment. Some time ago in the USA, a large tobacco company's account was up for grabs and every big advertising company was interested. There was a small advertising company owned by a fellow called Ben Duffy, and he was also trying to secure this account. He was up against some of the largest companies in the industry and it would be a coup to land such a prestigious client. Ben Duffy thought to himself, 'How am I going to get this account? I'm just an unknown player with a small company. There's no chance.'

But as he turned the issue over in his mind he realised there was a glimmer of hope if he concentrated on a commonsense solution. He thought, 'Let me put myself in the position of the tobacco company's executive. Let me think about some of the questions that might be on his mind.' He wrote out a list of 50 questions, and then narrowed those down to about 10 concise, insightful issues.

When he was being interviewed, he said, 'In preparing for today's meeting, I put myself in your position and thought there may be some things you'd want to know about me, my company, what's in it for you and what's in it for me. As such I've prepared a list of ten questions.' Well, the chap from the tobacco company replied, 'I've got ten questions here myself.' They swapped lists, six of the questions were the same, and Ben Duffy secured the account.

For years now, I've been using the Ben Duffy method. When I meet with a client for the first time, we go through the small talk and I let them speak about their past, present and future to establish rapport. Then I say to the client, 'You know, Joe, in preparing for today's meeting, I put myself in your position and thought there may be some questions on your mind. Who is Frank Furness? What is his company? How long has it been around? What's in it for me? What's in it for you? Are these some of the questions on your mind?'

There's always common ground here between potential client and aspiring salesperson. I then say 'What's in it for you? I just want to take a look at where you and your business are today and where you want to be in the future and see if we can help you get there with our products and services. What's in it for me? Well, I just want to develop the relationship so that, if you need our services either now or in the future, you'll know what's available.'

Now is the only time you will speak about yourself as you establish your credibility. This is an opportunity to sell yourself, your qualifications and your expertise. So if you've got a degree, if you've been in the business for 10 years, it's the time to broadcast it. After all, they may not know you or your organisation.

Bear in mind your body language, which at all times should be serene and non-threatening. The more relaxed you are, the better your body language will be and the more you will find a rapport with the client. Also, think about your choice of words. Don't use ambiguous language, and never stray into potentially controversial areas such as religion or politics, but also don't be bland and boring. Avoid using words such as *never* and *always*.

Prospecting

The key to success in selling is more to do with your prospecting ability than any other skill. Your success in this aspect of sales depends on three factors:

1. your ability to maintain high new-prospect **awareness** on a daily basis;

2. your ability to obtain the **information** about these prospects; and

3. your ability to **organise** the information.

You know it takes just as much effort to sell to a big client as it does to a small one; we just need to think way bigger than we currently do.

Many years ago, I took six weeks off and spent time going across America working with some of the top financial services businesses there to see how they functioned and what was effective about their operations. I was enormously impressed with a particular agency, since it had the most beautiful offices and luxurious cars parked outside belonging to the consultants. But more important was the method of working and prospecting that took place within the agency. There were a number of specialists in areas such as wills and trusts, pensions, and group schemes. These specialists were salaried staff who would go out on joint calls with sales consultants, providing a wealth of expertise and the average case size in this business was enormous. This was because sales consultants could aim for higher markets, secure in the knowledge they had specialists to back them up.

Here are some proven prospecting strategies which I use and have been shared with me by the tigers.

REFERRALS

The most successful people in sales are those who ask for referrals on a consistent basis. Ensure that you obtain at least three referrals from every satisfied client. Keep all of these organised in a book or on a computer system with a program such as Outlook, Act or Goldmine. You also have to put yourself in the position of clients and understand the psychology of why they don't like giving referrals.

The top reasons clients don't like to give referrals are the following.

- They don't want to upset friends and relatives.

- They feel that what they buy is personal in nature.

- They do not want friends to think they're being talked about.

- They may look down on salespeople.

- They may believe in the product but not want to be contacted by salespeople.

- They fear that the salesperson won't be there in the future.

- They may not know anyone to refer.

- They sometimes put people into class or income categories.

Q: **What is the best way to get referrals?**
A: Simply ask for them.
Q: **Why don't we ask?**
A: 1. We fear rejection.
    2. We don't know how to ask.

How to Ask

Always ask for referrals in a manner in which the answer will be a name and not a 'yes' or a 'no'. The *wrong* way of asking goes something like this: 'Mr Smith, do you have some names of people who may be interested in doing business with me?' The *right* way of asking can take several forms.

Referral Script 1

'Mr Smith, I find that all successful people have something in common and I'm sure you're no different. I've found that all successful people like to see other people grow, improve and become more successful. Mr Smith, who do you know who has just been promoted/relocated to the area/is a member of the local golf club/is your major supplier?' (And any other prompts that will suit your business.)

Referral Script 2

'If we were to swap jobs today, who would be the first three people you would call on?'

This script works incredibly well as there is no pressure.

Your Referral Prospecting Checklist

- List your 20 best clients.

- List the characteristics of your best clients.

- List your five worst clients.

- List the characteristics of your worst clients.

- What prospecting methods can you use to get more 'best clients'?

- List the 'best clients' you are going to phone in the next three days to ask for more referrals.

- When asking for referrals, ask for as many names as you can possibly get and then start qualifying them by getting more information on each name.

- Ask for permission to use the name.

- Contact the referral as soon as possible.

- Inform your client of the outcome.

- Prospect for referrers.

Three keys to successful referral prospecting are: integrity, informing your clients what they should expect from you, and telling your clients what you expect from them, specifically, referrals.

Did you know that only 42 per cent of sales and business people ask for referrals? Don't be shy. Clients are flattered when you ask for referrals. They have just purchased your product, they trust you, and they trust your company. They want to help you!

The benefits are enormous. As one tiger confided, 'I have referral systems that are so good I don't need to waste time and energy on any other form of prospecting.'

CENTRES OF INFLUENCE

These are people who may not even be clients of yours but who like you and your business and want to support you. They could be schoolteachers, secretaries or anyone else with whom you can develop a business relationship and who could be passing on potentially excellent leads to you. Identify as many centres of influence as you can. Find out about them, their interests and their hobbies. Then ask yourself, 'How can I help them in their business?' Once you have that information, act on it; they will act to balance the debt.

Do Unto Others

I knew a very successful general insurance broker who had an incredible client base that I really wanted to access.

Every time I asked him, he told me to get lost. I then thought about turning things around and giving to him first, knowing that the law of reciprocation would kick in. I asked him out for lunch on the proviso that we wouldn't discuss business. At lunch we discussed his favourite subjects: his two sons and his football team.

That afternoon I went back to the office and realised that five of my biggest clients had opened new businesses so I telephoned them and recommended this insurance broker. Subsequently, they all became clients of his. A month later he invited me to lunch and afterwards we went back to his office. He had 2,000 leads for me, and, even better, he had written to all of them to introduce me.

NETWORKING

Networking means attending meetings run by organisations including the Chambers of Commerce, Toastmasters, chief executives' groups or anywhere else where you can build your profile, meet other business owners and exchange business cards. If you stick by the basic rules, networking can have a huge impact.

But, pleasant as these occasions may be, don't forget that you need to 'work the room'. The biggest mistake I see at networking meetings is people speaking to and socialising with those they already know. If you're going to attend a networking meeting, set yourself a target of meeting a certain number of new people, speaking only to strangers. It's challenging and also entertaining.

My advice is to join two or three of these clubs. You also have to approach their meetings with a different mindset. If your approach is, 'Who can I meet and sell to immediately?' you might find yourself a little isolated. On these occasions it is important to play the long game. Go with the attitude of 'Whom can I meet with areas of common interest? Whom can I help with their business and whom can I make a new friend of and build a relationship with?' Remember, many of these people will not be potential clients or even need your product or service, but if you make a friend they could become a centre of influence or refer business to you.

Success comes more from attitude than ability. Whenever you meet someone new and build a relationship, your chances of success increase because of their vast network, which you may have access to sometime in the future. When meeting strangers, always get people to speak about themselves (the most important person in their life).

Some effective networking questions

- What is the best thing about your business?

- What are some of the unique features of your business that set you apart from your competitors?

- What are some of the biggest changes that have taken place in your industry over the past few years?

- What makes you so passionate about your business and is the real driving force that makes you so successful?

- How do you go about finding new business?

- How do your customer service and products differ from your competitors'?

What to do before you attend your next networking event:

- Ask the organisers to send you the delegate list beforehand. I always do this and most of the time they will oblige (after all, it is a networking meeting). Now I can study the delegate list and target those that I would want to meet before I go to the meeting.

- Find out who the key people to meet would be.

- Set a target to meet six (or more) new people.

- Don't spend all your time with people you already know.

- Mix and meet with strangers.

- Be proactive and engage everyone in conversation.

- Take plenty of business cards – many people forget this basic rule.

- Take a small notepad and pen to make notes.

- Take some breath fresheners and deodorant. There is nothing worse than speaking to someone with bad or coffee breath (what is it about these people that they always want to get close to you?).

- Arrive early and see if you can assist the organisers – possibly at the registration desk. This will also help you to strike up conversation with the key people that you'd like to meet.

- If given a name badge, wear it on the right side so that when you shake hands, your badge is in their direct line of sight.

- Remember, people would rather do business with someone that they have met at a networking meeting and developed rapport with than a cold call with a stranger.

Your Elevator Speech

Whenever you are at a networking meeting or even a social occasion and you meet someone new you start a conversation. The stranger would normally ask you what you do; your answer is your elevator speech. It's called that because it's designed to contain sufficient information to generate business during the short space of time you might share an elevator. You should be able to describe who you are, what you do and how you can help them (what's in it for them). It communicates in brief how you add value, benefit or quality to your potential client. Your elevator speech must be concise and you must know it so well that the words just roll off your tongue so you could repeat it in your sleep.

You must also distinguish between an elevator speech, which sells you and how you can help other businesses or people, and a statement, which will inspire no further conversation.

Introductory statements that are not elevator speeches include:

- 'My name is Michael and I am a financial consultant.'

- 'My name is Mary and I work as an accountant for XYZ.'

- 'My name is David and I'm a marketing consultant.'

None of these statements stimulates conversation and will either drive potential clients to the other side of the room or evoke in them the response, 'So what?'

Remember, every potential client is thinking, 'How can you help me in my business?' If anyone can say, 'So what's in it for me?' after your elevator speech, you are selling benefits.

So ensure your elevator speech runs along the following lines:

- 'My name is Michael and I help clients with their mortgages/ help them retire early/maximise their investments.'

- 'My name is Mary and we help clients with proven, practical ideas so that they can increase their profitability.'

- 'My name is David and our organisation helps businesses improve the way they promote and market themselves, so that they can close more sales and find more clients in a cost-effective manner.'

Remember, your goal is to keep the conversation going and to stimulate a response from the person you are speaking to. Your goal is not to talk about yourself and what you do but it is to find out what the other person does and what is important to them, in other words, to find out what's in it for them.

To prepare your elevator speech, first identify how you can help your potential clients.

List at least five things that you could do to help your clients, and then list five reasons why people should be doing business with you.

The Cure for the Common Voicemail

These days we are constantly plagued by voicemails and they often leave us in a quandary about whether or not we should leave a message. Try using your elevator speech the next time you leave a message and it could be something like this: 'Hi, Mr Jones, this is Frank Furness on 8526 039 051, and I help businesses to improve their Internet security so that they cannot be attacked by hackers or people who can access confidential information. I would like to meet with you and was wondering if I could take a few moments to tell you a little more about what I do. I'll try calling you again on Monday to see if we can get together late next week. My phone number again is 8526 039 051 and I'll be in the office for the rest of today and tomorrow. I'm looking forward to working with you.'

- Speak slowly and clearly so that they can understand what you are saying.

- Leave your telephone number twice, once at the beginning of the message and again at the end. This makes it easy for them to write it down.

- State the purpose of the nature of your call so that they know why you're calling.

- Leave a time when you're available for them to phone you.

- State what it is that you would like them to do.

Know Your Customer

Do you sell to clients the way they buy, or the way you want to sell? We know that people prefer to do business with those they like and trust and with whom they feel comfortable. In short, they like to buy from people similar to themselves. One of the most powerful courses I attended some years ago was about dealing with different personalities and being able to adapt your selling style to suit the client's way of buying. It made me realise that everyone is different and great salespeople have to be versatile. It's up to the seller to recognise various styles immediately and adapt so that it is easier for the clients to want to do business with us. There are many styles and substyles, but I am going to highlight just four.

STYLE 1: TASK-FOCUSED BUYERS

These buyers are normally decision makers or CEOs. They will arrive at a decision quickly, because their time is precious, and will buy from you only if you solve their problem or meet their expectations. They can often come across as demanding and pushy, less concerned with the relationship, more centred on the task.

Many years ago, my friend Alan Roets managed to secure an appointment with the CEO of a large corporation in South Africa. Alan entered the huge office while the CEO was on the phone. Rudely, he gesticulated to Alan to sit down and, when he finished his phone call, without any introduction or small talk, said, 'I need a million dollars' life insurance, beat that.' With that he threw a pile of quotes across the table.

Calmly, Alan walked around the table and threw the quotes

into the bin. He sat down and said to the CEO, 'Those are only quotes. This application is the real thing. Please complete and sign it and we'll get everything moving.'

The CEO glared at Alan, completed the forms and told him to leave. This was a huge amount of business for Alan, which he nailed because he was wise enough to know how to sell to a task-focused buyer.

- Impress them by *getting to the point*.

- Ask questions that *are relevant*.

- Support their *actions*.

- Demonstrate your *experience*.

- Make benefits *tangible and concrete*.

- Show commitment by *getting things done*.

- Be impressed by their *strength*.

- Best close: be *direct*.

STYLE 2: RELATIONSHIP-FOCUSED BUYERS – ENTHUSIASTS

These are my favourite buyers because I'm one of them. They are sociable, enthusiastic, friendly and normally not that concerned with the facts, figures and technical details. Many are sales-people themselves and impulse buyers. When they buy a product they will not normally read the manual, but try to figure out for themselves how the product works (ask me, I know – I have a cupboard full of bits left over from make-it-yourself models).

Some time back I visited a client who runs a successful business exporting machinery. He is very creative and has every gadget under the sun. I love gadgets, so for the first hour that was the topic of our conversation. When we finally got down to business he told me that he had been approached by his bank and his accountant, who had advised him to make a large investment that could save him tax and benefit his business. They gave him reams of technical data (which he never looked at) and left him to decide. Totally confused, he understood only that he had to make the investment. As we had been doing business for many years, he asked me to place the investment. I won a huge sale because I did not try to confuse him with facts and figures, but explained in very simple terms how this could benefit him.

- Impress them with your *flexibility*.

- Ask questions that *support their dreams*.

- Support their *ideas*.

- Demonstrate your *originality and creativity*.

- Make benefits *innovative*.

- Show commitment by *giving fresh ideas*.

- Be impressed by their *achievements*.

- Best close: be *direct*.

STYLE 3: SECURITY-FOCUSED BUYERS

These buyers will come to you only if a strong relationship exists and they trust you implicitly. They want guarantees and assurances and need to know that you are always accessible to help them. There's always a lot of small talk and relationship building before doing business. Frustrating at times – they normally don't make decisions quickly – they will become loyal clients.

When I first started in selling I sold an insurance policy to a counter salesman at an electrical store. Every month I had to remind him to pay his premiums and we became friends. When he went through a messy divorce, Candice and I invited him for supper and gave him what support we could. Soon after that he started on his own as a small electrical wholesaler, which very soon became a multimillion-dollar business. Every piece of insurance business for him (and most of his staff) was placed through me. This was the result of our having a very strong relationship and my being around during the divorce when other friends abandoned him.

- Impress them by *friendliness*.

- Ask questions that are *non-threatening*.

- Support their *feelings*.

- Demonstrate your *warmth*.

- Make benefits *personal*.

- Show commitment by *working with them*.

- Be impressed by their *loyalty*.

- Best close: *assumptive*.

STYLE 4: DETAIL-FOCUSED BUYERS

Think of engineers, accountants, computer analysts and any detail-focused professions, and you will normally be dealing with an analytical or detail-focused buyer. You can't sell to these people in the usual way. They will analyse, research and buy only when they feel they have explored every possibility. When dealing with this type of buyer, realise that they like to buy from specialists, so ensure that you know what you're talking about and have as much relevant data with you as possible.

This is the total opposite of my style, yet, when we moved to London, my biggest client base was dentists and computer analysts. As I know their buying patterns, I was very successful and they referred me to many others in their profession who saw me as a specialist. I would always give them an abundance of data and a few different options as well as sufficient time for analysis. Then I simply asked which option they felt was the right one and the business would follow.

- Impress them by *thoroughness*.

- Ask questions that are *detailed*.

- Support their *thoughts*.

- Demonstrate your *detailed knowledge*.

- Make benefits *provable*.

- Show commitment by *being systematic*.

- Be impressed by their *status*.

- Best close: *detailed summary*.

What this is really illustrating, is that you must be like a chameleon when selling. Very quickly recognise what type of buyer you are selling to and change your selling style to suit the way they buy, not the way you sell. For instance, let's say you are an over-the-top enthusiast. You will need to tone down and have a lot more facts and information than you would normally feel comfortable with if you are dealing with a detail-focused buyer. Remember, people like to do business with people similar to themselves whom they like, trust and feel comfortable with.

Making an Impact

There are many ways to market and promote yourself, but the creative approach always pays dividends. It's what makes you stand head and shoulders above the crowd. However, few people have been as creative as Gavin Sharples, a motivational speaker from South Africa who took to the stage for the first time in his career without wearing any trousers.

He told me how the trouserless technique came about. 'I went to an event where a group of speakers were before me,' he explained. 'I was just starting out as a speaker and I wanted to be remembered.

'Each speaker had to introduce the next. I asked the guy in

front of me to pretend he knew me. He introduced me as a personal friend who swam with dolphins so I knew the audience was expecting a back-to-nature kind of guy.

'Without thinking too much about it, I took my pants off. I had a long jacket on so all you saw was my knees. When the noise in the audience died away I asked, "Have you ever left home and thought you'd forgotten something?" Four months later CEOs who weren't even at the event were walking up to me saying, "Glad to see you've got your trousers on today."

'The impact it made stayed with me for a long time.'

Warming to a theme, he developed a package of breakfast sales talks for clients – and turned up in his pyjamas. His reputation for being out of the ordinary took a knock when he met a CEO one day who was bitterly disappointed to find him in a suit and tie. 'I thought you were different,' he moaned. After that Gavin wore long, baggy shorts, T-shirts, baseball caps and sneakers wherever he went to ensure he was always distinctive at work.

'I have created a brand and my brand is being authentic. I really try to do things with no airs and graces that will capture people's imagination. Everything I do is totally transparent.'

Another clever technique that has defined Gavin is that he sells his business card. Well, they are more paper holders than business cards. Nonetheless, he charges the equivalent of about £10 for them and sells them by the box.

'At first I did it because people said it was impossible to sell your business card. But who says business cards have to be on a piece of card? There's a money-back guarantee as well for anyone who uses the card to make a booking.'

Modestly, Gavin denies he is the best speaker in South Africa today. 'It wasn't my goal. In my view I'm not the top speaker: I'm just a person doing what he loves to do and hopefully turning lights on for people. I try to be one of the busiest speakers.

'It scares me when people hide by pretending to be something they are not. I'm trying to be genuine all the time. Hopefully I will inspire other people to be authentic too, by example. It is hard work, not glamorous but fun. For me it's a case of do what you love and love what you do.'

Although his style is 'live and unplugged', he always speaks with passion, whether his audience comprises top-level business people or nursery-school pupils.

Tried and True

Thinking creatively doesn't necessarily mean being extreme. There are other, more conventional, ways of tackling marketing and promotion.

TRADE SHOWS AND EXHIBITIONS

These are excellent places not only to promote your goods and services but also to spend a day or two walking around. Many people who are exhibiting their products could also assist your business. This is a good time to strike up conversations and see if they are a potential client, a professional introducer or a centre of influence. Do not approach them with the attitude of 'What can I sell them immediately?' but rather 'Are there any areas of common interest?'

NOVELTIES SUCH AS PENS AND CALENDARS

Everything about you or your organisation should be selling you in some form. Small novelties such as pens work well but an excellent alternative is the small A-framed calendar that you provide at New Year. Clients are studying their calendar at least twenty to thirty times a day and your name is in front of them every time they do it.

CHRISTMAS, BIRTHDAY AND SPECIAL-OCCASION CARDS

Everybody likes to feel special. Why not send cards to your clients, their partners or spouses and their children? Also, call your clients early on the morning of their birthday and congratulate them. Most times they will be in a positive frame of mind and this is a good time to ask for additional referrals or even to get together to review their own business situation. Remember to keep in touch with your clients all the time.

Promoting yourself

- Contribute time or money to a worthy cause.

- Sponsor a sports team.

- Give free speeches.

- Rub shoulders with the right people and doors will open.

PRESS RELEASES AND FEATURE ARTICLES

Build your profile and exposure in the community with articles in magazines and newspapers. There are thousands of publications in circulation. Find out which ones relate to your industry and area of expertise, write articles and submit them to the editors.

Some years ago I wanted to get some exposure through the columns of a newspaper. I approached the *Financial Times* with a view to having an article published in an international publication but was rejected. I persisted and eventually I had my own full-page column complete with my contact details in the newspaper for two years. I could not have afforded advertising on this scale, but a free full-page article resulted in huge amounts of business and helped to build my exposure globally. A lot of people look busy shuffling papers and playing with unimportant email while ignoring the important focus of marketing to clients

Always remember to include a photograph of yourself as well as your contact details. Find out who your biggest clients are and whether they have an in-house magazine. If so, get your articles published in their magazines as well. Should your organisation launch any new or updated products, have a press release where clients and potential clients can find out about these immediately. Remember always to keep building your profile.

MEDIA INTERVIEWS

Locate the local radio stations and make an approach, with a view to doing a radio interview. For the radio interview, be confident and prepared, and have three main points that you want to get across to the listeners. One organisation that I work with has a one-hour radio slot every week and this has built tremendous exposure for the organisation and keeps the phone ringing constantly. If your area of expertise fits in with any of the major television outlets such as Bloomberg, CNN or any local television stations, once again make an approach, since producers are always looking for interesting people to interview.

When I was a manager for a large life insurance organisation, I recruited a woman into the business, Renske Weihan, who was a real dynamo. Right upfront she told me that she was going to work only with referrals and her target market was going to be senior executives. She then went to a private wine estate and had cases of wine bottled bearing her name on the labels. Every time she delivered the policy documents, or when clients celebrated birthdays or other special occasions, she would take them a case of wine. As you can imagine, when these senior executives had dinner parties with other executives, questions were asked as to where the wine came from. This resulted in a huge number of referrals and, as a bonus, the wine estate became her biggest client.

Throughout the sales process, you should be continually:

- **asking questions;**

- **listening;**

- **qualifying;**

- **discovering hot buttons;**

- **building rapport;**

- establishing trust;

- developing credibility;

- developing a relationship;

- addressing objections;

- planning action steps;

- confirming the understanding;

- asking for referrals;

- evaluating positive and negative responses;

- affirming decisions and minimising buyers' remorse.

Technology happens, it's not good, it's not bad. Is steel good or bad?

ANDREW GROVE, FOUNDER OF INTEL

The great thing about a computer notebook is that no matter how much you stuff into it, it doesn't get bigger or heavier.

BILL GATES

I think there is a world market for maybe five computers.

THOMAS WATSON, CHAIRMAN OF IBM, 1943

Home is where you hang your @.

AUTHOR UNKNOWN

Not all problems have a technological answer, but when they do, that is the more lasting solution.

ANDREW GROVE, FOUNDER OF INTEL

Chapter 9

Technical Support

Typewriters are being consigned to history – and fountain pens, Filofaxes and fax machines are heading the same way. Gone are the days when office work was manual labour. This is the information age and, given the appropriate keyboard skills, the possibilities are endless. The most successful people in our business, the true tigers, are clued up on technology and reap the enormous rewards that it brings.

Technophobes are unlikely to be troughing at the top table in business – they simply can't compete. Anyone whose ability extends little further than email will likewise be left eating dust. Only those with a full grasp of cutting-edge technology can hope to compete for the big business prizes. And it's not an area in which many people can feel smug. Technology marches forward all the time at speed and any of the new programmes or recently created websites could make the world of difference to the way things work in your outfit. Now's the time to learn how to talk the talk as far as computer-speak is concerned.

The Vital Connection

Experts like Tom Antion put technology into perspective for people. It's his job to keep clients up to speed in this fast-moving arena. Here he's offering a few tips on some computer gizmos and all the bells and whistles they might possess.

'The great thing about the Internet is you can reach around the world from your desktop with low investment. It is a great time to be a small business. Some devices that will allow you to sell thousands of dollars' worth of goods and services are inexpensive or even free to download.'

He has sound advice for anyone contemplating a website. 'Get the proper attitude before you start. You should be thinking money, not pretty. Pretty does not sell. It drives no traffic. You have to have a good psychological sales process as fancy graphics are not what get people to pull their money from their pocket and give it to you.'

He offers some easy website rules for guidance. 'Make sure your pages are simple so people can get around them with ease and never feel lost. Ensure the copywriting on the page is done well. Sales copy pushes the emotional buttons that will have people reaching for their wallets.'

His chosen sales weapon is an advertorial. 'This is an advertisement that looks like an editorial or article. When it's presented in this way, readers don't approach the product with sales resistance. They don't have any reason to scroll to the bottom of the page looking for a price. I have one page on my website that has brought in over one million dollars because people have no sales resistance to it.

'Headlines are critical. I write a headline then I put all other headlines that didn't make it to the top in as subheadings. Instantly they offer lots of structured information to readers.'

His own websites are honey pots for Internet travellers in search of information on his chosen field, public speaking. They rate highly in the Google hit parade and here's why.

'About three years ago I spent a long weekend creating about 120 pages on my website all based around my expertise in selling on the Internet. I optimised – the term we use for making pages search-engine-friendly – all 120 pages to suit the search engines. So when someone types in public speaking the search engine can't help but give my site a high ranking. Be very specific with website pages and think in terms of more than one website, as it is very cheap to do nowadays.'

He has experimented with pay-per-click, a form of advertising used on websites and search engines. The advertisement appears when words are tapped into the search box, so it reaches a target audience. Payment is not due when the advertisement appears but when it is clicked.

'Pay-per-click can make you broke or be the best thing in the world. You can drive targeted traffic to your site and may be very effective, but only if you can close the deal with sales copy.'

He also offers cautionary words about shopping carts. 'Most shopping carts given free by a web host are totally a piece of junk. I compare it to a dumb cashier at a convenience store where you might get the right change if you are lucky.

'But a good technological shopping system is the equivalent of a professional sales force selling 24 hours a day, seven days a week, day and night. It doesn't take a vacation and doesn't get sick.'

One device to watch out for with a shopping cart is up-selling, whereby a second product is automatically offered upon the purchase of a first.

'You must have this function on a good shopping cart. I use kickstartcart.com, from which you can download an e-book to evaluate available shopping carts. Sometimes you have to throw out the old and come in with the new.'

A simple autoresponder can intercept and answer emails. But Tom uses a sequential autoresponder that not only sends a single response but numerous emails at whatever intervals you pick. It can be used to follow up sales, offer customer services and updates and even e-courses. 'I have a friend who does e-courses and never even talks to anyone,' he says. 'He doesn't do "webinars" in case the fear of its technological demands deters people. I only use teleseminars. In the first month of doing so I made $12 thousand. On one day I had 1,400 people on the line while I was sitting at home. I didn't even shave that day.'

He also runs 'butt camps' for clients – a little like hardworking boot camps, but it is all done sitting down. 'People's brains are smoking after a whole day.'

Further, he invites people to his home at Virginia Beach so his highly individual brand of intensive tuition can be up close and personal. 'I own the only facility of its kind in the world. My house has a theatre, a big screen in the office for audiences to watch while I teach, a high-speed wireless facility, a tennis court – in fact everything anyone could want both while they are being taught and when they relax. It is a tremendous experience and sells out instantly. Clients are immersed in the experience and get to grips with all the nuances.

'I also run mentor programmes or joint ventures. People pay a fee and I train them over the course of a year in exchange for a percentage of their profits. At first some people object. But by the time I have made my cash reward the customer has made three times more money.

'It's hard to learn about technology out of a book. It is especially worth investing the time and effort into learning about it for those who have a fear of the Internet and computers.'

A New Set of Tools

Not everyone can get over to Tom's place for top-level technology tuition, but there are plenty of other options. Many adult learning facilities offer excellent terms. So, if you're not already doing it, book yourself onto a course and learn how to use the computer effectively. Learn Word, Excel, PowerPoint, Outlook and any other programs that will make you more productive.

If you and your company don't already have **website**, question why not. Invest in setting up the best website you can afford. If you're going to be working with sophisticated clients, bear in mind that they will normally be up to the mark with technology.

Get the latest **handheld devices**, **BlackBerries** and **phones** and keep them with you at all times. Most of them now have WAP capabilities, which means you can dispatch faxes and retrieve or send emails wherever in the world you find yourself. There are plenty of other ways to invest cash when it comes to technology.

Digital recorders are now tiny and can store up to 44 hours' worth of material. Once you have completed a meeting with a client, dictate the notes into the recorder, connect it to your computer and download the sound file. This can then be used as a dictating machine so the information can be swiftly typed up. Alternatively, just listen to the recording on your computer prior to your next meeting to get up to speed with events. I have also used the digital recorder to capture client testimonials for my website, record interviews with tigers on leadership and entrepreneurship and record my new book for transcription.

The technology behind voice recognition is leaping ahead. I first used **voice-recognition software** five years ago and, thanks to my accent, my dictation would transcribe in gobbledegook. Now with the latest package (Dragon 9 Professional) I can put on my headset, speak at a fast pace and it will type automatically into Microsoft Word with about 95 per cent accuracy. The biggest secret with voice recognition is that you need to train the software to your accent and jargon by reading aloud. It's worth the effort. Soon you will use it to answer your email. Best of all, you can link your digital recorder with the voice recognition. Think of the possibilities! You can dictate into your digital recorder, link it to your computer and sit back as the recorder downloads the sound files, links up with the voice recognition and transcribes it into Word. How much time and money could you save? You now have a window for that extra game of golf – but don't forget to mark it in the diary as prospecting.

Business-card scanners are one of those natty devices that may well be worth their weight in gold. We are constantly attending networking events to meet potential new clients. Normally we return with a mountain of business cards that we aim to input into the database but never get around to it. The latest card scanners are tiny and function with 100 per cent accuracy and then export to whichever database you choose. The secret with networking is to get in touch with these new contacts as soon as possible.

Keeping in Touch

New technology can help you construct a 10-touch plan for all your existing clients, which means making contact at least 10-times a year. You can email, telephone, meet face to face or, better still, create an online newsletter or e-zine. Develop it on a monthly, weekly or quarterly basis for your clients.

This does a number of things: it keeps your name in front of your clients all the time and also helps to establish you as an expert in your field; it gives you massive online exposure and gains further credibility with your current clients; it forces you to package your knowledge into concise articles on a regular basis, which you can recycle for many other marketing uses. Take a look at http://www.frankfurnessresources.com/wizemail to see the software I use to produce my online newsletter. It comes with templates and is simple enough for anyone to use. It also gives me exact statistics on who opens the mail, who un-subscribes (no more free lunches for them), the click-through rate to my website and plenty more. If necessary you can print off the e-zine and send it to customers or potential clients as hard copy.

At every networking meeting that you attend or from every potential business contact that you meet, obtain permission to send out newsletters or e-zines to these people using the infor-mation from the business cards you have harvested.

As for the content of the e-zine, take note of the following points.

- Ensure that you have a main article that always provides a lot of information that your readers will find valuable.

- Have links to related articles and other sites that may be of use to your readers.

- Offer tips to your readers such as books, reports or anything else that can help them in their business.

- Market your own products, services and workshops through your e-zine.

- Have an editor's note at the beginning of each e-zine or newsletter.

- Incorporate power words.

- Have links to products that you want to sell.

- Offer testimonials from satisfied clients.

- Give real-life examples and show how you've helped clients.

- Use case studies: they always position you as the expert in your readers' minds more than your coming out and saying so.

- Jot down eight questions your clients have asked you in the past. Answer each one in a short article, as there may be many other clients who have the same questions in mind.

- If you have been to any industry conference workshops or seminars where you've picked up some helpful hints, share these with your readers.

- Offer a list of your top five to ten tips on a certain subject.

- Recommend books or resources and offer reviews on some of these books.

- Include stories and photos from clients.

In 2005, a friend, Herb Kelly, suggested that I start a newsletter, since I have so many contacts. I made a lot of excuses, saying that I wasn't any good at writing and did not have the time. Eventually, I relented and sent out my first newsletter to about 3,000 people. The very next day, I received a phone call from Singapore from someone who had been forwarded the newsletter. He said that he liked what he saw, then he enquired whether I could travel out to Australia and Singapore to train his two sales teams there. This turned into multiple assignments in Asia and, if I had not sent out the newsletter, I would have missed out on massive potential income.

It is also important to monitor your newsletter. My list has now grown to 15,000 subscribers and increases weekly. It is very important for me to find out how many people actually open the newsletter, how many unsubscribe and how many click through to my website

The Real Article

Perhaps the easiest and most inexpensive method to expose and build your brand is by marketing with articles. We're living in the information age and everyone is looking for it free on the Internet. How much free information are you putting on your website to attract potential clients (you must encourage them to sign up for your e-zine when they download the information)? You can also submit these to article directories (take a look at http://www.articlesubmittingsoftware.com).

When people download the articles and put these onto their sites, this now creates links back to your website which in turn ranks you higher on the search engines.

Articles work best with headlines – and this can be the hard part. How do you convert casual readers to your marketing brochures and websites without pulling your hair out with the time-sucking chore of producing a winning headline? I discovered a great piece of software that automates the process for you, take a look http://www.headlinecreator.co.uk. This is technology working at its best, taking the sweat and tears out of a tedious task and enhancing your final product.

Substance over Style

Once, not so long ago, websites were all about flashing logos and eye-catching animations. Of course, good design still counts for a lot, but today websites are centred on making your site easy and effective, a standard tool for increasing your business, improving service and reducing costs.

Flash movies, cute though they are, hardly achieve this. I have found from experience that there are three different types of people involved with developing websites: the first can design efficient and effective sites; the second has marketing experience and can turn the website into a marketing mechanism to attract new clients; the third knows how to attract visitors to the site. Rarely can the same person do all of these. Each strand is as important as the next. After all, you can have the best website in the world, but if no one sees it you are just throwing away money.

Also, remember to make it easy for people to contact you. The rule of thumb is that two clicks should bring website visitors any information they need.

Other Business Tools

It's the buzzword on everybody's lips. A *blog* (or weblog) is a journal kept on the Internet that quite simply keeps people in touch with the writer. Often blogs are updated daily and contain all the information that the writer – or blogger – intends to share with the world. The term also applies to websites dedicated to a particular topic that are updated with the latest news, views and trends. This is perfect for any professional practice. Set up your own blog for free at http://www.blogger.com or http://wordpress.org.

You don't have to be a technical genius to master *videomail*. The necessary software can be downloaded from the Internet free of charge. What does it enable you to do? Well, you can record a message or video and send it to the screens of other computers or even upload it to your website. The possibilities are enticing. You can follow up a meeting with an important client with a short video, thanking him for his time and highlighting what topics the meeting covered. Remember, clients appreciate instant response and this could be something that distinguishes you from competitors. I consult with CEOs in 48 countries and I know they like to do business with innovative, forward-thinking partners. It's time to tailor your business to suit.

My favourite piece of software for this kind of wizardry is called Camtasia (take a look at http://www.frankfurnessresources. com/camtasia).

Teaching and demonstrating visually is much more powerful than using words alone. But getting the right group of people together for a training or demonstration can be expensive and inconvenient. Camtasia Studio lets you easily create compelling training and presentations for web and CD-ROM delivery and you can do it without ever leaving your office. It is the only product versatile enough to record live PowerPoint presentations, personalised technical training sessions, and rich software demonstrations.

Consider the potential applications:

- **explaining** how to complete a difficult form or paperwork;

- **demonstrating** your latest products or services;

- a live PowerPoint **recording** with voice (at least you can hit the stop button if this is too boring);

- having a **frequently asked questions** section of your website where clients can watch videos of complicated questions – and plenty more.

In times like these fundamental business tools like brochures begin to look a little old-fashioned. And what happens when you get sent a brochure? I know that too often I file brochures straight in the rubbish bin, no matter how glossy the print finish or artful the layout. One alternative to expensive brochures that all too often go to waste is an *interactive CD*, which could include:

- video;

- audio;

- testimonials;

- brochures;

- contracts (and videos to explain how to complete them);

- meet-the-team section;

- client list.

These cost less than full-colour brochures and have a longer shelf life, since normally they will be passed from one person to another to watch. We're living in a multimedia society, so give clients the choice.

A couple of years ago, it would cost a small fortune to go to television studios to make a professional *infomercial*. Now you can use software such as Serious Magic to produce professional infomercials at your office for minimal cost. You could use these:

- to explain the implications of the budget;

- for inheritance tax planning.

The list continues.

I decided to spend a morning videoing 65 30-second sales tips. I now send these out to my subscribers and clients weekly to keep the relationship and add value to their business.

I took this one step further and submitted them to the online video channel YouTube and set up my own channel. All this cost me nothing. Take a look at http://www.youtube.com/salestips.

Within six months I had 100,000 people view my videos and this resulted in many people signing up for my e-zine, product sales and even speaking engagements I am now in contact with other potential clients that I would never have met before without the benefits of this technological era. If you are not using this medium, you should ask yourself why. Large and small organisations as well as politicians have all seen its potential to reach millions of people and are now using it.

I send my e-zine subscribers a short 30-second marketing video mail each week using this software. It differentiates me from my competitors and adds value.

How about having *teleseminars* or 'webinars' for your clients, wherever they may be, once a quarter? It feels up close and personal and yet you never leave the comfort of your office. In essence you provide a telephone number and a time to your customer. At the appointed hour you broadcast a teleseminar. You can even include a Q&A session at the end of the seminar, once again adding value. Your clients can choose whether to take part or not.

Don't overlook the advantages of *free international telephoning*. If you are using broadband, you can download http://www. skype.com, which will allow you to telephone anyone else with broadband anywhere in the world for *free* (I love that word). You can also have a conference call with three other people. I recently conducted a conference call for two hours from my office in London with CEOs in Dubai, Indonesia and Hong Kong, all for free. Calls can even be recorded. Even better, if you both have a webcam you can see each other.

I also wrote a number of articles and submitted them to online article directories. At the bottom of each article I put in my details and a link back to my website. This has resulted in over 2,000 links back to my website and a high Google rating. Take a look at http://www.articlesubmittingsoftware.com.

The people who get on in this world are the people who get up and look for the circumstances they want and, if they can't find them, make them.

GEORGE BERNARD SHAW

In the midst of winter I finally learned there was in me an invincible summer.

ALBERT CAMUS

Our greatest glory is not in never failing, but in rising every time we fail.

CONFUCIUS

In order to succeed, we must first believe that we can.

MICHAEL KORDA

By changing your thinking, you change your beliefs ...

AUTHOR UNKNOWN

One person with a belief is equal to ninety-nine who have only interests.

JOHN STEWARD MILL

Success consists of going from failure to failure without loss of enthusiasm.

WINSTON CHURCHILL

Chapter 10

Belief, Change and Focus

Millionaire W. Mitchell lives by one simple code. 'It's not what happens to you,' he says. 'It's what you do about it.'

The words are common sense, of course, and roll easily off the tongue. But they are all the more compelling because they fall from the lips of a man who has nearly died in two appalling accidents that have left him scarred and paralysed. This is a man who practises what he preaches.

Mitchell was a fast-living free spirit when he jumped on his new, high-powered motorbike one day in 1971, heading to his girlfriend's place. He had recently left the Marines and was enjoying a new job as grip man on San Francisco's cable cars.

A collision with a truck turned the shiny machine into a ball of flames with Mitchell at its heart after the motorcycle petrol tank's cap spun off. An estimated two and a half gallons of fuel was ignited by the heat of the engine. It was only thanks to a quick-thinking passer-by armed with a fire extinguisher that he survived at all.

The accident left him with severe second-, third- and fourth-degree burns. Every day he was in ceaseless, excruciating pain. Although his head and his torso were largely unscathed – they were protected by his helmet and leather jacket – his face was horribly scarred and his hands were reduced to stumps. When he passed the gates of an elementary school children rushed over and chorused 'monster, monster'. He understood why they were chanting, for he himself was deeply shocked when he saw his face for the first time after the accident.

But the constant stares from city folk wore him down. Eventually he moved from San Francisco to a small town in Colorado, where he found people more ready to accept him. A few years down the line found him a happier human being.

'Not only had I become successful financially, having started a major new business, but I had become successful emotionally,' he recalls. But his trials were not yet over.

Disfigured he may have been but he could still pursue his need for speed by becoming a pilot. A little more than four years after the motorbike disaster he was taking four friends from Colorado to San Francisco in his light aircraft when it stalled 30 metres (100 feet) in the air, due to ice on the wings.

The aircraft plunged to earth and landed belly up. As his friends crawled away from the wreckage Mitchell discovered he couldn't move his legs. Injuries to his spine sustained in the crash consigned him to a wheelchair.

'My face looks like a badly made leather quilt. I have no fingers. I cannot walk. The average person might call me the unluckiest man alive,' says Mitchell.

And for a while Mitchell succumbed to the notion that he had suffered more agonising pain than anyone deserved. 'My whole world was filled with impossibilities,' he remembers, as he wrestled with the physical difficulties posed by wheelchair travel. Finally, the internal resources that served him so well after the initial crash came to the fore once more.

'Before my accidents I could do 10,000 things. Now I can do

9,000 things. I can either spend the rest of my life focusing on the 9,000 things I can do or instead dwell on the 1,000 things I can't do,' he explains.

In addition to his business successes he has been a politician, sits on numerous boards as a director and became an environmental campaigner, a media personality, a political commentator and an international public speaker. His hobbies continue to include river rafting and sky diving.

He determines to make us all see things from a different perspective and uses the analogy of a baby taking its first steps to make his point.

'[At first] the baby does not succeed, hits its head, smashes its face, looks ridiculous and the whole process is downright dangerous. In fact the baby fails and fails – If you choose to call it failure.

'Then one day he or she will take a first step. It's not failure, is it? It's called learning to walk. They are not mistakes – they are experiences.' Faced with crises, he insists that 'they either shut you down or you make it to the goal line'.

Mitchell has another mantra that smoothes his passage through life, which he has also used throughout a successful business career. 'Do whatever it takes.'

As he looks back at his eventful life, he has no regrets. 'Would I trade what I've learned? Not in the world.'

Mitchell's self-belief ensured he did not wash up as a failure on life's shores. He's not alone. Look at some of the other greats who have had conviction and belief in what they've done. Composers including Wagner and Debussy were booed, hissed and ridiculed at their early concerts but they kept composing until they were successful.

You have to be brave to have a belief and, if you're brave, that belief leads to a conviction, and that is the courage to overcome any obstacle, focus on what is important and achieve your dreams.

The Lessons of Failure

Tigers like Mitchell are remarkably resilient. If failure happens – and it does – then they acknowledge it and learn. They've got this ability to try and try again after things have gone wrong or after they've made mistakes or experienced failures. They re-group and attempt it all over again.

The admission that, well, we failed is hotly followed by the assumption that it was a learning experience. Every failure is viewed as an opportunity to improve. When others have been knocked down they stay down. Not so with the tigers. The top producers have been knocked down – many of them have been flattened many times – but they have the ability to get up, overcome rejection and then start doing the things that the others won't or don't. Henry Ford once said that failure is the opportunity to begin again more intelligently. The term *bounce-back-ability*, coined by football management, is equally applicable to business.

Footballer Frank McClintock is an example of a tiger who refused to lie down. When he transferred from Leicester City to Arsenal FC in 1964 for the record-breaking fee of £80,000 he assumed he would soon reach the heady heights of success. But in 1967 Arsenal lost in the final of the FA Cup to Leeds and the following year the team were defeated by Swindon. Television coverage of the occasions shows McClintock a dazed figure wandering among the purposefully marching military bandsmen. When he got home he threw the losers' medals in the rubbish bin.

He was down in the dumps for several days before deciding to take action. Famously, his determination paid dividends. In 1971 McClintock was captain of the Arsenal team that won the double – the FA Cup and the League – the first time the feat had been pulled off for a decade. In charge of the back four, McClintock played alongside football heroes including Charlie George, George Graham and goalie Bob Wilson. In 1970–1 he was named Footballer of the Year and in 1972 he was made an MBE. McClintock was respected by fellow players for his never-say-die attitude. Despite the gut-wrenching disappointments he had experienced, McClintock worked out what was needed to achieve success and set about it with vigour.

Mark Victor Hansen is famous today as the writer and co-founder of the publishing sensation *Chicken Soup for the Soul*, a book that's sold 60 million copies in North America alone. It's spawned more than 100 sister titles and is published in at least 37 languages. Yet motivational speaker Mark was turned down by 33 publishers before getting into print. 'Our agent fired us. We went to the Book Expo and got turned down by another 134 people,' he told me.

Mark didn't break stride. Despite the mountain of rejections he and his partner kept getting. 'You have got to do butt-breaking behaviour that no one has ever done and come up with unique markets,' he said.

Guess what. Mark is an avowed goal setter. He set a target of selling a 1.5 million books in 18 months and saw the goal achieved. 'I teach people to have 101 goals written down, although I have 6,000. I always have ten outrageous goals,' he explained.

When you learned to ride a bike as a child you were nervous and you probably fell off more than once. But it didn't stop you climbing back on and having another go until you had mastered the skill.

The Courage to Change

It's difficult to deal with people who are hung up on the notion of failure. Also, I find it hard when I encounter people who are closed to new ideas. I keep hearing phrases such as 'This is not going to work for me'; 'This worked for them only because they were lucky'; 'I don't stand a chance.' Time and again I am haunted by that horrible phrase, 'I can't.'

It's astonishing the number of people who refuse to make changes in their outlook, their behaviour or their business plans when all the evidence screams that they should. After all, somebody once said the definition of insanity was to keep doing the same things and expect different results.

Sometimes the change needs to be groundbreakingly big, a new product, better premises, a different country. Usually, though, some tweaking is sufficient to fashion the necessary forward momentum. A number of incremental changes can add up to a whole new business plan if you let it. Here are a few ways that you can make small changes that will have big effects.

Be proactive rather than reactive. Think of the advantages – it means you have the power, the freedom and the ability to choose appropriate responses rather than accepting the same old ones.

Reactive types have a few telltale stock phrases. It is always somebody else's fault – their company's, their manager's, the economy's. But really it's not, and now it's time to remind you of one of my favourite sayings: 'It's all about you.' Yes, *you* have to take the blame when things go wrong but also *you* take the credit for the triumphs. *You* are the architect of your successes as well as your misfortunes. Ask yourself, can I change? Do I acknowledge that I am personally responsible for all that I have, all that I do and all that I am?

There are plenty of people out there not willing to learn or change. Make sure you are not in that number. If you suspect you might be, then it's time to do something about it. Think about the kinds of books you are reading. The range of advice and motivational books written by me and others is mind-bogglingly large.

Don't have time to read? You can listen to CDs or podcasts and improve yourself while you work or travel.

Be willing to learn from other people, especially those who have achieved in areas where you would like to leave a mark. Analyse what it is that makes them different.

Unless you are prepared to change, things are going to stay exactly the same as they were last week, last month or last year.

Is there anything you've always wanted to do but found a mental barrier? Conquer your limiting beliefs. Change the words you use to 'I can', 'of course', 'I will'.

Try something for 21 days and it then becomes a habit. Think of one thing you can do right now, a habit you can change, for the next 21 days.

Just Do It

Sometimes you have to change your attitude, your habits, your friends, the way you approach work, the way you think about things. You see, successful people are implementers. Exploring, studying, investing don't produce any success without implementation. Implementation draws a bold line between massive success and failure. We've all found great ideas, gone to great seminars, listened to great programmes and done nothing with them. Some people have implemented a few small changes and then seen staggering results.

So think about it. Resolve today to implement one idea that you've been thinking about, and *do it now*. Remember, the implementers, the doers and those who are prepared to change are the achievers who enjoy massive success. You really just need the discipline to do it.

I learned the hard way a few years ago when I was running a sales seminar in China. Afterwards, everybody in the audience came up for a chat in the usual way. Each of them handed me a business card, which I thrust in my pocket, said goodbye and began talking to the next person.

After about five minutes the chairman of the host company asked me why I had insulted everyone he had invited there that day. I was mystified until he told me that when the Chinese receive a business card they hold it in two hands, study it, feel it and examine both sides. It's then common courtesy to reciprocate with a business card, once again holding it in both hands.

That experience taught me the importance of changing my behaviour to accommodate other cultures. I've since discovered the Chinese take business seriously, so now I begin seminars there by giving the audience permission to laugh and have fun.

I carried out some swift research among the top Chinese insurance brokerages and sales consultants to discover what they believed to be the keys to success. The qualities they rated most highly were persistency and consistency. Then came professionalism, evident in their impeccable dress, punctuality and ongoing educational studies.

Next came hard work and this is quickly apparent to visitors. The Chinese are among the hardest workers I have ever known – in the office early, not leaving till late. In descending order the other qualities they deemed important were listening and communication skills, discipline, confidence and honesty.

I made a similar mistake on a trip to Japan. Every time I spoke I was greeted with *'hai'*, a word I took to mean yes. I thought negotiations had gone extremely well until I spoke to a friend more acquainted with Japanese culture than I.

He pointed out that *hai* can mean yes, no or I don't know. Its approximate translation is 'I see you and I hear you.' So perhaps I didn't do so well on that occasion after all. Crucially, though, I changed so that doors to the vital Chinese and Japanese markets could open.

As I said before it is all about you. Nobody is going to do it but you.

FOCUS OF A TIGER: DAVE WILLIS

After change comes focus, the quality that will clinch success. And for many focus must act like armour plating to help achieve those dearest ambitions. Whenever you take risks, be prepared to be criticised by your friends and family. But be prepared to take those risks and stay focused. The worst thing that could happen is that you don't get where you hope to be. The best thing that could happen is that you get there, in spite of everything.

This is another quote from a company that I have been working with for some time, which is hugely successful, and the man who leads it is a dreamer and an achiever. This is what he says: 'I'm fully focused on the task at hand and do not have more than one major objective at a time. When focused on an objective, I will not likely consider or investigate any other opportunities that may take my focus off my main objective.' Like all tigers he has a dream and he goes for it!

There are a number of companies and tigers that have made their special mark on me, but one that really stands out. I spoke to a CEO group a few years ago, and in the audience was Ann Willis, who was a managing director. She invited me to speak at the group's conferences in Europe, America and Asia, and that was where I met her father Dave. He founded the Whitford Worldwide company, makers of fluoropolymer coating used on cookware and in industry, and, at the age of 61 at the time of writing, he is still the top salesman, CEO and one of the most energetic and fully focused people I have met. This is his story.

Shortly before Christmas in 1968 I was fired as a sales manager. I was 28 years old, had four children, a big house and not much money. I was determined never to be in that vulnerable position again. The company accountant had been fired the same day and the only option as we saw it was to start our own business where we could control our own destiny. We might fail, but it would be on our terms, not someone else's.

The oil industry, centred in Houston, needed the product to coat studs and nuts for flanges, pipe lines, pumps, valves, offshore and down-hole equipment. We called on the stud and nut producers and then made joint calls with them on the end users. In a relatively short period we were specified by nearly every Gulf Coast oil and chemical facility.

It took some time to build a strong senior management team. Not everyone wants to take a chance on what is by any measure a small company. It takes time to convince people of the credibility of a company as small yet as diverse as Whitford. We have our own people in 14 countries, we manufacture in seven of those.

In building the team, we have also concentrated on the technical side of our business. Over the past seven years we have added many technical skills in the form of about 15 PhDs with very diverse educational backgrounds. Along with the people we have added superb analytical capabilities particularly suited for our markets.

What has resulted so far is a group of people who get along well, actually have become friends. This group works hard and plays hard. Long days coupled with an occasional long night. The result is the ability to talk out difficult problems on a non-personal basis.

I hear about business plans, exit strategies, burn ratios and many other of today's 'sophisticated' business buzzwords. We had none of these then; we have only a smattering now. We do not and did not 'fly by the seat of our pants'. We concentrate on the opportunities at hand; try to make the most of them by converting them to sales and profits as quickly as we can. We have become slower at this as we have grown.

We do not do sales budgets. A sales budget is simply the end point of an argument between the budgetee and the budgeter. How low can I get away with versus how tough am I going to insist on what I think they can do? We make all comparisons versus the previous two years. We chose two years because, if we have had a tough year, the following year's comparisons can look like more progress than really occurred.

Going forward I fear for our ability to find people willing to take some risks, make some mistakes and get on with it. I see a real reluctance to take risks in the younger generation that we count on to carry the business forward. That may be the attitude of anyone my age, but I don't think so. Every decision seems to be based on what is the least-risk path. This, in my mind, is seldom the least risk and may well be (cumulatively) the most risk.

I am fortunate to have a daughter completely capable of running the company. She is the one who faces the task of getting good hard-working risk takers to continue the growth and diversification of the company.

I try to listen, put myself in the place of the customer, try to figure out what we can do that the competition can't, what story can we tell that our competition can't (or doesn't)?

I have pretty good product knowledge as I have been here from the beginning, but what I really do is to sell as a business person. What problem(s) do you (my customer) have that I can help you with? What else can we do to sell more to the same accounts? That includes of course trying to replace products they are buying from others.

Before starting Whitford I was the sales manager, actually the only salesman, for a very small company in the plastic-compounding business. The company had been established for several years and sold [to] all of the US. This was my territory. Many of the accounts had never been called upon. I had never been to many of the cities.

Without a lot of thought, I simply picked a city (Chicago, LA and Houston were where most of the accounts were), bought a plane ticket, rented a car, spotted the locations of the customers on the rental map and went to see them. Planned the day with the most distant customer first so that I could get there early, using the pre-business-day hours to travel. And then work my way back to the hotel as the day went on.

After a short while, I had a fairly standard trip that took me to Chicago for two or three days, San Francisco for Thursday evening and Friday for sales calls and the weekend. Then on to Los Angeles for three or four days, usually back to San Francisco, where I spent the weekend with my college roommate, and then to Texas for one or two days and home. I spent less time on the road, but still covered the country.

I do what I can to learn the habits of my customers. Los Angeles was great, as I could see one of my customers for breakfast, another for lunch and then take a six-pack to one late in the afternoon that almost always went into dinner. I would fill in the rest of the day with other accounts. I was able to make five or six *good* calls in one fairly long day.

When we started Whitford I did the same thing, just to different accounts. First, in the US and then added Asia on much the same basis. I would leave the US to arrive in Hong Kong on Saturday night; two and a half days there, then to Kaohsiung (southern Taiwan) late Wednesday and work my way north with our agent. Two calls in Taipei on Saturday morning, the 2 p.m. Pan Am flight to Tokyo with a connection to LA.

At that time a business-class ticket allowed you as many stops in the

US as you wanted as long as you were proceeding without backtracking. I would then go on to Houston and home. I made that trip four times a year. Later I added Singapore between HK and Taiwan. Sales calls resulted in sufficient business to put our own person in place in Hong Kong, which is central to the area.

After establishing some rapport, I would ask for leads from them. Where are you having problems? What could be better about the coating? What else did they need? They were generally very receptive.

Basically we followed our customers around the world. We first went to the UK. That was easy: we had an Englishman working for us and he wanted to return home after graduating (MBA from Wharton), so we put a little money in to get him started and, the next thing we knew, we had a base in England. This was 1970, the year after we started in the US.

I would go to England several times a year to make calls and bring the Europeans up to date on what we were doing in the States. Our original partner in the UK was not a particularly good salesman, but a good technical manager. After about a year we hired a sales manager, which made a substantial difference.

He then saw Germany as the big industrial market in Europe, so he and his wife learned German, moved to a large home with a basement that was converted to an office and storage area. We then had an office in Germany. That gave us good access to the German-speaking countries, including East Germany.

Black and Decker moved their small-appliance line from PA to São Paulo, Brazil, in 1985. We found an individual who was retiring from a small-appliance business and hired him to form a Whitford company. The initial plan was sell our products and then to manufacture locally, which was accomplished over about a year.

From about 1973 we had been going to Asia to sell to that market, which, while geographically large, did not have huge business. It was growing in Hong Kong and Taiwan. By 1984 we had a Whitford company and an office in Hong Kong, along with a local manager. We established agents in many of the countries. We put an American in HK in late 1989 to better oversee the entire area from Japan to Australia.

Establishing a factory in Singapore in 1993 was a natural step. It gave us local production that our competition did not have for nearly another 10 years. When the Asian financial crisis hit in late 1997 it was a great help to us, as we offered two-week delivery when our competitors offered two-month delivery. This reduced our customers' inventory in transit, saving them substantial letter of credit commitments and expenses when the commitments were particularly hard to get.

Many years ago, soon after Whitford was founded, we wrote down our thoughts about the kind of company we wanted to be, the principles that should guide us, the kind of environment we wanted to create for our people. We boiled these down to six simple statements and we printed them. Called 'The Whitford Ethos', these are displayed in all our offices around the world. This is what the Ethos says:

1. We believe in making superior products. Our products must be better than those of the competition in some way: properties, price, or both. This makes it easier for the customer to choose Whitford – and harder for him to choose a competitor.

2. We believe in serving our customers better. While we sell products, we are in the business of people: people whose jobs may depend on the support they receive from their suppliers. In times of diminishing product differences, service can set us apart. We must place our customers' interests above our own. It is difficult to fire someone who serves you well.

3. We believe in leading the way. We must commit a higher percentage of our sales, interest and talent to research and development than our competitors do. We must blaze new trails.

4. We believe in high personal ethics. No lying, cheating or stealing. We despise politics, the pastime of small people. We embrace equal opportunity: everyone must have the same right to succeed.

5. We believe in being happy. We spend a lot of time at our jobs. It should be happy time. Life is short. We agree with the Scottish proverb: 'Be happy w'er leevin, for y'er a lang time deid.'

6. We believe in divine discontent. Self-satisfaction is the first step toward failure. Remember: 'Good enough is not good enough.'

FOCUS OF A TIGER: JUDY BLAIR

I recently spoke at a conference in Phuket and one of the partners in the business, as well as the top salesperson, was Judy Blair. She told me how she changed her life after reaping the rewards of being highly focused.

I loved travelling and after graduating I decided to roam the world for a few years. I ended up working as an underwater filmer, which I loved as long as I was able to film new things and continue to travel to new places. However, meeting my husband meant I could no longer keep travelling, and then I quickly got bored of filming the same thing. I had also grown decidedly bored of the low pay! I decided it was time to look for a 'proper' job.

With a degree in economics and a master's in finance, I wanted to use those skills in Thailand, where I was living at that time. Through a series of coincidences, I met a man based in Singapore at his beautiful house right on the beach in Phuket. He seemed to have the perfect lifestyle, a beautiful house, enough money to enjoy the fine things in life and yet he only worked three to four days a week. It all sounded too good to be true and so after a bit of digging I discovered he was the top salesperson at his company.

My mind works quickly and after concluding this was the perfect job for me I asked immediately how I could get his job. I told him my background, he called his boss and soon after I had an interview.

I was offered a three-month trial, no pay, and commission only. They had little to lose! I don't think anyone in their Bangkok office was impressed at his recruiting backpackers from the beach. I didn't pay much attention to them and they obviously didn't think I'd be around for very long.

Structure and organisation have always been important to me. The job was straightforward, they told me, and as long as I did what needed to be done I would succeed. 'It's a numbers and activity game,' they kept saying. I was told to come in each morning at 8.30, make as many calls as necessary to set up 10 meetings a week.

I did this every day religiously. I saw many people and things seemed to be going well. My boss was confident I would have my first deal within a few months. Three months came and went, four months, then five and still no deals. For the first time in my life I started to question my ability. I had never failed at something I was so absolutely determined to achieve. I went to my boss to ask what I was doing wrong. He said I was making more calls and seeing more people than anyone else in the office. He joined me in a meeting to check what I was doing, after which he maintained I was doing the job right and should just hang in there. So I did.

Then, as my confidence reached a new low, my first deal finally came in on 17 September 2001. Four more came in that week, and three each week until the end of the year. I ended up writing US$60,000 and winning Best New Starter for the year.

The next year I wrote over US$200,000 and won Top Sales Consultant and Top Case Writer that year for Thailand. I maintained those positions the entire time I worked with that company – purely through sticking to the formula that works. It really is 'a numbers game'.

The postscript to this is that Judy then started her own company – the one featured at the convention where I spoke. It's now a very successful company, and Judy also has a stake in a huge organisation in Indonesia.

Street Smarts

I learned an important lesson a few years ago. I was speaking in Mumbai in India and was staying at the Taj Mahal hotel. It was glorious. I had a suite with four rooms, complimentary bottle of wine each day and a butler at my disposal. That all ended when I stepped outside, and saw poverty like I've never seen before. Little children were dressed in threadbare clothes, no shoes, illiterate.

I love shopping, so hired a taxi and drove into the shopping area. As we stopped at a traffic light, I looked out of the window and saw a sea of children holding their hands out for money. One little girl particularly caught my eye. She was about five, barefoot and waiflike with big brown eyes that penetrated my soul. I put my hand into my pocket, pulled out some money and started opening the window. The taxi driver shouted at me, 'Don't give them money, they are beggars.'

The light turned to green and he started driving. The kids scattered except for the little girl, who started running next to the car. I said to the taxi driver that she would be killed – there was so much traffic on the road including cars, buses, motorcycles and the occasional cow. He replied that she knew to run close to the car, as we would soon be stopped by another traffic light. As soon as we stopped, there were a new lot of hungry faces with this little girl right at the front. This went on for some time and eventually I told the taxi driver to pull over and I gave her some money.

If ever I feel sorry for myself now, I think about that little girl. She didn't give up, used the obstacles to her advantage and persisted until she was rewarded. My biggest reward was to see her beaming, smiling face as I gave her the money. She may not have had much going for her, but she had positive attitude and enthusiasm in abundance and I've never met anyone so focused anywhere in the world.

The World's Best Waster

One of the tigers who responded to my questions confessed to being 'a rotten waster working part-time'. But the rest of his answer shows how he had brought down his barriers to usher in success.

'I do no more differently than I would be doing in any other business. I seek out the individuals with needs, identify, analyse and detail the areas of common interest, offer solutions and finally encourage and conclude corrective actions.

'It never worries me to earn less today, as there's bound to be more tomorrow. I always put clients' needs first as there's no business as easy as repeat-referral business. I don't mind working from 8 a.m. to even after 10 p.m. four days a week, ten months a year, in exchange for the lifestyle and returns we achieve.

'Having said that, much of the work is more than work only. It's socialising, meeting people, friends, opening doors, learning, loving a good life and more.'

Here's someone who enjoys every minute of what he's doing.

- Be brave, have belief.

- Every failure is an opportunity to learn and to improve

- Focus is the armour that protects you on the road to success

Conclusion

There's so much to say about achieving success in the business world and it's my job to phrase it in memorable terms. Now it is time for me to fall back on acronyms and the first one I'm going to throw at you is the DOT principle. The letters stand for *determination*, *optimism* and *toughness*, three qualities that will take you a long way up the company ladder.

And here's another. Tigers have realised that if you want to make more cash, you need the right KASH. Here's how it's made up.

K stands for *knowledge*. Have you equipped yourself with the best knowledge, of your product, market, competitors and future trends? The Internet is a wonderful vehicle for collecting information.

When I first started selling in 1980, I managed to make an appointment with a CEO in a huge organisation. When I walked in he told me that he was going to give me the biggest order of my career and I could see myself retiring the next year. He then started asking me technical questions and I stumbled, didn't know the answers and told him I would have to go back to my office for the information. After a few minutes he grew tired of my excuses, walked around the table, shook my hand and said, 'Young man, go away and learn your business. In five years' time give me a call and let's see if your knowledge is up to scratch.'

I left there feeling depressed, dejected and deflated. Yet it was a great lesson for me because after that I vowed never to have that happen to me again and knowledge became one of my greatest assets.

A stands for *attitude*. This is arguably the most important attribute in tigers. They have an incredibly positive attitude, no matter what happens. In 2006, I was booked to make a presentation on marketing and technology to a law firm during a lunch break. When I arrived all the staff were cheerful and enthusiastic – except one. She came in muttering about having to give up her lunch-time. When they brought in lunch, she found something wrong with everything. All throughout my talk she kept shaking her head negatively and during question time stated that she was already so busy that she would never have time to use the technology to save her time. Afterwards I asked the managing partner what she specialised in and he replied, 'Taking days off.' If she thought her poor attitude had not been noticed then she was sorely mistaken.

I had a totally different experience when speaking once in Kansas City. I was booked into the wonderful Raphael Hotel Country Club Plaza and the porter introduced himself as Michael, showed me to my room and went out of his way to be genuinely helpful. I told him that I drank gallons of water and felt that the prices they charged in the hotel room minibars were a rip off. I asked him where the nearest supermarket was so I could buy some water. He told me not to worry and disappeared. Ten minutes later there was a knock on my door and Michael stood there with a huge packet filled with bottles of water from the local Seven Eleven. As he had bought this from his own money, I asked him what I owed him, to which he replied, 'Nothing sir, just glad I could help.' As you can imagine, he ended up with a healthy tip. I was so impressed with his attitude and, by this token, he has scaled the heights of success.

S stands for *skills*. What kind of training are you giving yourself and your staff? When I work with members of the Olympic team I am amazed at how receptive they are and at their willingness to learn. No matter how able, they are always working on improving their skills. We need to be doing the same.

When I was managing a large sales force I had one salesman who just could not close sales. I told him that I wanted his attitude to improve, although it was already great. He became the most enthusiastic person in the office – still no sales. I told him that I wanted more sales activity. He was the busiest, most motivated person in the company. Still no sales. I then decided to go on a joint call and observe him in action. He was so enthusiastic that he never knew when to shut up. He spoke himself into a sale and then right out of it. With some coaching and learning the skill of keeping quiet and slowing down, he went on to become of the best salespeople in the team.

H stands for *habits*. Tigers have developed the correct habits. Tiny bad habits can start to grow into *bigger* bad habits and affect work. Being five minutes late for appointments, bad breath, BlackBerry addiction (I saw someone checking his emails during a movie the other night), dirty shoes, dirty nails – all small things that can have a huge effect on the business.

One of the top achievers that I knew in South Africa, Alan Roets (we met him in Chapter 8), was an extremely creative thinker and this was how his day worked. His first appointment would be at 7.30 in the morning. Why 7.30? Well, most of his clients were top executives and from 9 o'clock they were either flying around the world or were tied up in meetings all day. At 7.30 they could all meet with him. His next appointment was at 9.30 and his third appointment at 11.30. This he did five days a week and anyone who has 15 appointments a week in industry will always be successful. He was a master delegator who passed all administrative tasks onto his extremely efficient staff.

His next appointment during his working day was at lunch-time, and every day he would take one of his clients out to lunch – but there was a proviso. This client had to bring another potential client to the table with him. As these were top executives, he would socialise with them for an hour and a half and they would then return to work. Three in the afternoon was golf time and every day he would play-partner another of his clients provided they brought along two others to make up the four-ball. Can you imagine, at the end of each day, he had seen, mixed and socialised with three new people. He didn't have to do any prospecting because they would normally end up as appointments in his diary; and, because he was working in a market with top achievers, he would always be referred to other top achievers. Isn't this a creative way of working? Can you imagine having lunch out every day and playing golf every weekday of your life and on top of that earning a lot of money? What a lifestyle!

Finally, here are some wonderful quotations from some of the tigers who responded with information that has assisted me in the research. I hope you find this 'tiger talk' as inspirational as I do.

Once a year, go someplace you've never been before.

Enthusiasm – enthusiasm is an infection that reaches everybody who comes into contact with it. You can't operate without it and you can't invent or learn it. Ninety per cent of the struggle to find it involves being in the right business for the right reasons.

Have the courage to think big. No one would remember Alexander the Average.

A loving atmosphere in your home is the foundation for your life.

Live a good honourable life, then, when you get older and think back, you'll be able to enjoy it a second time.

Take into account that great love and great achievements involve great risk.

Have the courage to take all of your inadequate skills, resources, experience and people and then start fighting to make it happen, and, even though you'll fail time and time again to the point of defeat, get up off the ground and survive.

I believe you must have a burning desire to achieve, tears in your eyes and an ache in your heart; you must want it so badly that it hurts.

Open your arms to change but don't let go of your values.

Take the competition seriously but not yourself.

Believe in people and they will believe in themselves.

Resources

Frank's Net resources

http://www.frankfurness.com
http://www.frankfurness.com/closingscripts.cfm
http://www.frankfurness.com/free_downloads.cfm
http://www.frankfurnessresources.com

Sign up for Frank's monthly newsletter and weekly video sales tips at http://www.frankfurnessresources.com/newsletter

Book Frank to speak at your next event.
Email: events@frankfurness.com

Recommended Websites

http://www.antion.com
http://www.articlesubmittingsoftware.com
http://www.astronautspeaker.com
http://www.cobrabeer.com
http://www.gavinsharples.co.za
http://www.headlinecreator.co.uk

-dubai.com
http://www.rudyinternational.com
http://www.teamhoyt.com
http://www.terrybrock.com
http://www.~~~~~~~~~~~.com
http://www.vmitchell.com
http://www.youtubestrategies.com
http://www.ziglar.com
http://www.alvinlaw.com

Recommended Books

Bayan, Rick, *Words that Sell*

Collins, Jim, *Good to Great*

Freiberg, Kevin and Jackie, *Nuts*

Godin, Seth, *Purple Cow*

Kennedy, Daniel, *The Ultimate Sales Letter*

Mandino, Og, *The Greatest Salesman in the World*

Parinello, Anthony, *Selling to VITO*

Rackham, Neil, *SPIN Selling*

Richer, Julian, *The Richer Way*

Weiss, Alan, *Million Dollar Consulting*